THE
life

audit

THE
life
audit

Take control of your life now
Every minute counts

Caroline Righton

HODDER
MOBIUS

For Ben and James

Copyright © 2006 by Caroline Righton

First published in Great Britain in 2005 by Hodder and Stoughton
A division of Hodder Headline
This paperback edition published in 2006

The right of Caroline Righton to be identified as the Author of the Work has been
asserted by her in accordance with the Copyright, Designs and Patents Act 1988

A Mobius paperback

1

A CIP catalogue record for this title is available from the British Library

ISBN 978 0 340 92444 0
ISBN 0 340 92444 6

Book Design by Janette Revill

Printed and bound by Clays Ltd, St Ives plc

Hodder Headline's policy is to use papers that are natural, renewable and
recyclable products and made from wood grown in sustainable forests. The log-
ging and manufacturing processes are expected to conform to the environmental
regulations of the country of origin

Hodder and Stoughton Ltd
A division of Hodder Headline
338 Euston Road
London NW1 3BH

BE SENSIBLE

Whenever we examine our lives in detail we will experience a variety of emotions, some intense. The author has had only positive feedback from those who
have done the programme, but if you feel in any way vulnerable or upset, do
stop the Audit and seek help from your doctor. The Life Audit is advisory only
and neither the author nor the publisher can be held responsible for actions that
may be taken by a reader as a result of reliance on the information contained in
this book, which are taken entirely at the reader's own risk.

Acknowledgements

I'd like to thank the many people who helped, encouraged and supported me during the development and writing of *The Life Audit*. First, of course, thanks to my husband, Mark, who bore the auditing of our life stoically. Thanks too to the rest of my family, including my father Patrick and especially to my sister Elaine for her love and conviction, from the very start, in me and the concept. I'd like to thank Charlotte Barton and Jon Roseman for their friendship and constancy through the writing days, along with David and Scilla Grose for their unequivocal support and practical advice.

What has become *The Life Audit* has been a long time in the making and has been shaped by many experiences good and bad, and by landmark friends and colleagues. These include Michelle Sammons, Des Weston, Francoise Drew, Bob Clarke, Mary Quicke, my team at Carlton, Jane McCloskey and Peter Gregory, Jim and Sue Kane and Steve and Suzy Pass. I suspect some of them won't know what they did or said but should not underestimate how a throw-away comment or the smallest action can start a chain of thought or bring about a change in attitude! I owe special thanks to Tod Grimwade, Grace Kitto and Claire Stevens for their encouragement and the part they played in the development of the idea.

Thanks to Sue James' enthusiasm about my own Life Audit story and her subsequent publication of an article about it, Fanny Blake introduced me to my agent Jane Turnbull, who saw the plan as the book it has become and who has been wise and supportive throughout. The whole team at Hodder, including Rowena Webb and my editor, Helen Coyle, have been tremendous.

Finally, a big thank you to all those who had a go at Life Auditing and let me tell their stories. You know who you are – your contribution has been invaluable. Thank you.

Contents

Introduction

S itting in bed very early one January morning, hugging a cup of coffee, was the moment I realised that I'd run out of excuses as to why I wasn't living the life I wanted and felt I deserved, and why the happiness and contentment I sought seemed to elude me.

Those 'excuses', the ones I'd used to stop me following all my dreams, had walked out the door ten minutes earlier. Two sons returning to their own life adventures at college, and one husband who was starting a job at the other end of the country, had all left together in a cheerful post-Christmas chaos of luggage, hugs and promises to ring later in the week.

Sitting there alone, I pondered that in life terms I seemed to have everything. It was just that I seemed to have forgotten where I'd put it. It was 5a.m. on a Monday. The week stretched ahead of me with no one to fuss about, to be distracted by or to eat up the spare-time hours of each day that stopped me from doing . . . from doing what? There was the rub! Although, at that precise moment, bleary-eyed and reeling from the departure of my much-loved chaps, I couldn't and didn't articulate what it was I wanted to do. I knew deep down that not only was I no longer sure about what I wanted, I didn't even really know at that moment who I was either.

It took longer than those first minutes alone to recognise the scale of my ignorance and bewilderment, but right then I did subliminally understand that I was at a pivotal moment that represented either enormous opportunity or a terrifying abyss into which yet more years might vanish, with the 'real me' never surfacing again. I experienced a sudden urgency to seize the moment and make every second from now on count. Really count.

There are moments in life when everything just comes together. Life deals you a hand of cards and gives you a chance. Such moments are as much the result of serendipity and coincidence as of design or effort. They are rare, and while you are blinking into the blinding opportunities they offer they can disappear as speedily as they came. I was determined that that was not going to happen, that I was going to be accountable for my own fulfilment, and that I was going to come up with a plan that would shake me out of indecision, apathy or fear and force me to be a conscious player in my own future.

I'm a businesswoman. I like the clarity of a good, concise business plan. I don't like flaky indecision – I like order and making informed decisions. I prefer to know how bad a loss might be, while at the same time wanting to aim for optimistic targets that are realistically achievable. I like checks, controls and schedules that ensure plans are on course. I like routine and I love the grids, charts and spreadsheet documents that help me run my businesses successfully.

I decided to approach this life crossroads in a businesslike way, and what became evident very quickly was that the currency at issue was time. Not in terms of how much time I had wasted in the past, but how much free time did I have in the future to do something with? How much time was committed to 'must-dos' such as work and sleep and family and friends? How much time did I have left over? How did I use my time? Who owned it? Was there enough left over to realise a dream?

At work I'd know exactly how to tackle the problem if I

was faced with having to apportion funds to a new business project from my existing budget. I would look closely at expenditure elsewhere to see if there was any unnecessary spending, or if I could make some savings to free up the disposable money needed. The equation would read X (Total Income) – Y (Committed Expenditure) = Z (Disposable Income). Y would have to come under close scrutiny to see if the figure could be reduced to a lower breakeven amount without having an adverse effect on the business.

Wouldn't it be interesting if, instead of grumbling that I never had enough time to do this or that, I could establish exactly what I *had* to spend time on and see how much was left over?

> **X (Total Hours Available) — Y (Hours Committed) = Z (Time Available)**

X was an easy number to fill in, with either 24 hours for a day, 168 for a week or 8760 for a year. All I had to do was to work out what figure Y was and what I wanted to do with Z.

Y had to be the events, people and things that were non-negotiable, concrete commitments in my life, so these should be easy to identify. Simple addition would come up with the hours they needed, to leave me with the surplus hours (Z). A happy by-product of the process of eliminating the non-essential and time-wasting elements in my life should be a clearer perspective on the dreams and ambitions that could be realised by using Z to progress them.

Introduction

Taking this rationale further, I could then treat each wish, ambition, dream or even regret, however small, as something I wanted to invest time in, and actually plan and keep account of the amount of investment I was making. This would be proof that I was not being passive but was putting in effort and hopefully, step by step, was getting nearer to achieving some of my ambitions.

Does any of this connect with you? Are you now, like I was that January morning alone in bed, excited at the prospect of getting some perspective on your life? Do you feel that the way you are living could do with an overhaul, needs a bit of consideration, would benefit from some informed analysis? And aren't you indeed the best-placed person to do just that?

Ask yourself these questions:

- *How much time do you spend thinking about the things you are going to do one day?*
- *How much do you let yourself get bogged down in things that have to be done?*
- *How often do things just happen – and you just react?*
- *How rare is it for you to make things happen in your life?*
- *Do you feel other people and their needs totally dictate your day-to-day life?*
- *How often does a moment pass – such as the moment you could have gone travelling, changed career direction, left a lover, had a child?*

Each one of us has times of change in our lives. These can appear as opportunities or crises, but in fact are nearly always a little of both. They happen to everyone – male or female, young or old. At that moment, aged 45, I was facing a crossroads, but I'd also had significant moments of crisis and opportunity earlier in my life.

Are you:

- *In your late teens or early twenties, leaving education and trying to decide what career to follow?*
- *Trapped in an unfulfilling job or facing redundancy?*
- *In your thirties and worried about relationship commitment or the noisy ticking of the biological clock?*
- *An empty nester who now the chicks have flown, thinks your marriage and life look barren?*
- *Retired and facing acres of empty time on your hands?*

When my husband and sons all left home at the same time I found myself living a life that I hadn't prepared myself for at all. My overwhelming desire at that time was to shout, 'Stop!' to the world, to my life, and to everyone I knew or cared about. I wanted to stop events overtaking me, and I desperately felt I needed time to come up with a plan or a strategy. I knew I was lucky. I felt I had a million blessings to count – a loving, healthy and happy family, good friends, a good job, a lovely home and every day packed with activity. But I was also aware that when I was on my own (and I was suddenly alone a lot at that time), despite my good fortune I was restless and troubled. I'd been too reliant on the distracting, defining business of being a mother and wife to realise that I was, frankly, lacking any personal direction. I'd so loved being Mum and looking after the family as my sons were growing up that, outside work, I'd not attempted to do anything else. It had been a packed and fulfilling life so far. But, undeniably, I now had no real sense of excitement or optimism about what life ahead held.

I didn't want to be labelled a clichéd mid-lifer, because I knew I'd been at similar life crossroads before. At 19 I'd had the dilemma of whether to take up a university place or head straight into journalism. At 33 I'd had to decide whether or not to pursue a lucrative opportunity, and at 39 whether to have the third child I felt I wanted. I knew I'd been lucky in that each time things had worked out well, but on this occasion I didn't want to wait for events just to 'happen' – I wanted to take control of my own destiny.

With my sudden and strange change of circumstance I longed to talk to someone who would understand and be wise and totally honest with me, but although I know therapy is hugely helpful for many people, personally I couldn't bear the thought of dealing with a therapist who wouldn't know me from Adam and might be tempted to tick the Mid-life Crisis box straightaway. And there wasn't enough wine in the world, it seemed, to turn my friends into my personal, intimate and honest life coaches.

The brutal truth that I eventually had to face up to was that I knew myself all that needed to be known about my wishes and regrets and about what made me happy or sad, and that all I had to do was to ditch the self-denial and be big enough to face up to those truths. I realised that if I could do that then maybe I could solve my own dilemmas, properly identify the opportunities heading my way and not be either a bore to my friends or a cash cow to well-meaning but anonymous therapists.

So how did I start? I felt I must treat myself as a stranger whom I needed to get to know better, and take a really good look around myself and my life. Who I was, what I felt, what I did and with whom. I decided to do a Stocktake on Me and, working on the premise that I was the best-placed person to know my innermost thoughts, to try to become my own therapist.

And so the Life Audit was born. It's worked for me. It's worked for the people who have tried it. One person described doing the Life Audit as like 'looking into a magic mirror' that bounces life's answers back at you. Another told me he felt he'd taken an 'honesty drug' and that it was like meeting 'a whole new person' hiding inside him.

The findings can certainly be surprising. Auditing my life revealed, to my surprise, that I was bored at work. Up to that point I had thought I loved every aspect of it. I had a job in television, commissioning and working on great programmes, based in one of the most beautiful parts of the country. But the corporate treacle that went with the post was deadly dull and tedious and had really worn me down. I wasn't frustrated or angry with the limitations of my job as a TV Controller. I was in fact plain bored. It was recognising that the lethargy in my limbs mirrored the apathy in my mind when looking at what lay ahead of me each working day that ultimately made me give up my well-paid and creative but ultimately boring job.

The Life Audit started out as straightforward Time and Activity Accounting, and I am deeply grateful to the scores of people who helped my original principle evolve organically into its present form. While they were looking closely at how they spent their waking hours they didn't have the benefit of all the charts, instructions and information contained in this book. Each person, to a greater or lesser degree, used the basic system I had designed to create his or her own bespoke version of Life Auditing. In many cases their feedback altered the emphasis of the questions contained in each section of the Audit to prompt your thinking. Their contribution to ideas for saving time and improving Breakevens was enormous.

Some volunteers only looked at one part of their life, others dissected every minute and cross-referenced them to make detailed Stocktakes, and some just asked and answered the questions. But all were enthusiastic, and the stories related in this book represent their input and experiences as they audited their lives.

- *'It was a chance to reconcile some issues.'*
- *'It gave us the confidence to start up our own business.'*
- *'It forced our relationship problems out in the open.'*
- *'I've decided I am going to have a baby.'*
- *'I'm giving up my job and going travelling.'*
- *'I've forgiven my brother.'*
- *'I've forgiven myself.'*
- *'I've stopped complaining and now see how happy I actually am.'*
- *'I'm no longer so scared of the future.'*

These are just a handful of quotes from those people who have put their lives under scrutiny. Starting with the day-to-day mundane issues we all have to deal with, they have managed to bring order and supply answers to all other aspects of their lives too.

You are about to take charge of your own life. It's a very straightforward plan, very practical, and will be very personal to you. Everyone is different, with individual dilemmas and circumstances, hopes and dreams. The Life Audit doesn't pretend to provide tailor-made answers that you can look up in an index, but it does contain lots of practical anecdotal tips that have worked for me and for others who have audited their lives. This book, therefore, is a guide to help you identify who you are and who you want to become. You are going to be the one addressing your innermost thoughts, and only you will know if you choose to ignore them. One thing I can tell you is that you *will* know.

Right, enough encouragement! On with the practicalities. The basic premise of the Life Audit is that life is 'time', or rather life is what you do with time. You go to bed happy or sad, fulfilled or bored, depending on what you have done with the waking minutes of that day. A certain amount of your time will have been spent doing things you *have* to do. The Life Audit addresses every aspect of life, right down to the organisation and contents of your sock drawer, to find out why you might feel time-poor.

Ask yourself these questions:

- *Do you career through your weekends 'getting on top of things', just so you can launch chaotically into the next week?*
- *Do you try to pack a week's worth of training into one extended session at the gym and feel dreadful afterwards?*
- *Do you never have anything to wear because you haven't found the time to sort out and coordinate your clothes?*
- *Do you end up having fillings because you missed two years of dental check-ups?*
- *Have you lost contact with good friends because there was never enough time to keep in touch, and instead find yourself spending time with people you neither particularly like nor have anything in common with?*

If your answers are all or mostly 'Yes', you are just like me and millions of others. Life is pretty damn short, and all of us wish at some time that we had more control – that we could stop the world and just think and plan a little and perhaps as a result make life better, not only for ourselves, but maybe for others too.

You are going to come up with a strategy that will change things – it will make you and the events in your life happier, make you more fulfilled, let you feel less guilty and enable you to be more in control. The Life Audit gives you back control because you have to think of time as the currency of life – sleep time, work time, leisure time and so on – which gives each use of time its own 'value' in making up the life you choose to lead.

The Life Audit is a system that calculates the way you use your waking hours and helps you to 'add value' and 'make time investments' so that every minute counts . . . even the ones when you just flop in front of the telly. It's an interactive accounting system that offers you the opportunity to do a thorough and serious stocktake of every aspect of your life – whether it's the state of your sock drawer or how many hours you've managed to spend with your children. This Life Audit will ask the big questions – on relationships, work, health, soul – and will offer new ways of thinking about the ruts and patterns that we all fall into. With the Life Audit's help, you will start to dump the baggage and clear the decks for a new you and a new life.

What is an audit?

I n its primary sense an audit is an official examination and verification of financial records. It's made up of a statement of accounts and a balance sheet that are drawn up following a methodical and detailed review of how a business has operated. There have been several recent scandals in the world of high finance after auditors uncovered all sorts of discrepancies when carrying out their examinations of corporate accounts, and that's what an audit is all about. An audit confirms, or not, how a company thinks it is performing. An audit flushes out any fraud, discrepancy or over-optimism in the book-keeping, and may force the management to face hard facts.

The word 'auditor' has an appropriate double meaning. As a financial functionary it is of course that person who conducts the audit of accounts. Its other meaning is that of a hearer or listener, because the word 'audit' comes from the Latin *auditus*, meaning 'hearing'.

Because *this* audit is a self-assessment of your life you won't have an independent judge to verify your findings. But no matter, because you are the best person to hear those innermost nagging doubts, worries, secret dreams and ambitions that you don't ever articulate to anyone else. Also, you know there is absolutely no point in lying to yourself about them. This audit will erase them or help you to make the time and find the space to allow them to blossom and change your life for good.

Quite simply, you are going to look at every aspect of your life, armed with checklists and assessments of how much time and value you allot each area. You are then going to start coming up with informed priorities and identify the areas that are ripe for pruning or elimination.

Let's use the sock drawer analogy again. Say, currently it has a mismatched collection of various hues, singles and inappropriates. After the audit it will contain *exactly* the number of pairs of socks you need for the occasions requiring socks, in *exactly* the right colourways, neatly paired and taking up *exactly* the amount of physical space they need and *exactly* the minimum amount of thinking or management time in your life.

You will apply the same principles to all other aspects of your life, using a series of grids and questionnaires designed to assess the current situation. You will then have the information to set a basic requirement of time and energy, called a Breakeven, and finally you will be able to identify areas of opportunity, growth or enhancement. All this will be accompanied by the case studies and experiences of other people just like you who have audited their own lives.

The process can take however long you want it to – a week, a month, a quarter. It took me four weeks to get the proper measure of my life and to stocktake all my belongings, relationships and other life issues. Then I established the Breakeven position that I was happy with in each area. This operation has now become an ongoing process of adjustment which I carry out twice a year as my circumstances and ambitions shift and change.

Why audit your life?

I first used the expression 'life auditing' when a faded photograph of an old friend fell out of a book I was lending to someone. They asked who it was and I said quite glibly, while ripping up the photo, that he was someone I'd known ages ago but that I'd audited him out of my life. The person I was lending the book to was quite shocked, and I admit my attitude must have felt cold-hearted. But it was true. This incident had occurred just as I was assessing my life, and any friendship I'd had with the man in the photo had not been one I intended to make any future investment in. That decision had been made when I'd looked closely at all my friendships, new and old, and had worked out how much time I could spend on each in terms of being a good friend and nurturing those relationships. He and I hadn't made grade, and the issue was one of 'time'. The ripping up of the photograph made it seem like the brutal amputation of a friendship. In fact the relationship was long dead and buried – we'd had no contact for years. Sure, his picture is still part of a photo collage of that era that hangs in my kitchen, but our paths had ceased to cross and he had obviously felt as inert as I did about keeping the lines of communication going.

It will be up to you to choose how brutal or otherwise you want to be about the time and attention you give to friendships on the wane. But keep in mind that the Life Audit has to be predominantly a positive experience – for instance, it would be a bad idea to be too judgemental about five friends if you only have five friends! This exercise is really as much about balance as about elimination.

A final word, therefore, on the audited friend. Should our paths ever cross again, I'm quite sure we'd be pleased to see each other and would reminisce and be interested in each other's fortunes. I do hope, however, that having done the Life Audit I wouldn't resurrect a long-term commitment to keep in touch unless our reacquaintance warranted it. In other words, I hope I would have achieved what I regard as the right balance.

Most people these days understand the difference between cash in the bank, credit limits, planning for the future, realising assets, being in debt and, most importantly, what they'd do with a windfall! Taking the language and management of money as the analogy, then, the real poverty many of us seem to experience is that of time. We are all time-poor and that type of poverty, just like real hard cash poverty, stifles, paralyses, dulls us into inertia, keeps us in our muddles and prevents us from realising our true potential and letting our lives grow and become more enriched.

So instead of pounds or euros, think units of time and what you do with them. Add them up and see how much is left over once you've spent the time needed for basic survival. Have you enough to invest in a plan, a dream? Are you making your time work hard enough for you? Is how you spent your time giving you back a decent rate of interest to justify that chore or activity? People who get in a mess financially do so for many reasons. But chief amongst them is being chaotic and not keeping a close account of what they earn, spend and borrow.

The Life Audit is all about assessing your life and then conducting an analysis on everything so you can become an informed player in your own existence. Don't feel shamefaced if the chaos you are in has allowed any or all of your life to spiral so far out of control that you are not sure where the days and weeks go. Most chaos is born out of optimism. Just like the retail junkie who can't help overstretching on a store card and sincerely believes he or she *will* be able to make the extra payments at month end, so people who end up chasing their tails, frantically trying to keep on top of their busy, overscheduled lives, honestly think that they *will* be able to make time to do X or see Y. Sadly, they rarely do. But carrying out the Life Audit changes all that and gives you a much better chance of making everything change for the better.

A three-stage process: the Life Audit principles in brief

The first thing to do is to inject some realism into that optimism, and that's why you will be filling in charts and answering questions that will provide you with all the facts you need to make informed decisions. There are charts at the back of this book, which are the ones I and others use when we are life auditing. They are the basis for The Life Audit programme as explained throughout this book. You can photocopy them or use them as examples to create your own versions. If you want a pristine, designed A4 stationary set of all 48 charts, personalised with your own name for unlimited printing off, sign up to The Life Audit website for a small fee. This membership also allows you to enter data online confidentially. The data is used to generate colourful charts and graphs of your time use, calculated automatically for you each day. All membership benefits can be found at www.thelifeaudit.com. Whatever option you choose, make sure you have at least one week's worth of daily records such as the time sheets and day journals, and clip them into a ring binder.

GETTING STARTED – BASIC NEEDS

- *A set of charts*
- *A ring binder and hole punch*
- *Pencils*
- *An eraser*
- *A pocket-sized notebook*
- *A pocket calculator*

Always write in pencil and have an eraser at the ready. Apart from the inevitable occasions when you write something down and are then shamed into changing it because you know it's a fib, there will also be times when something gets entered in the wrong column or your addition is suspect – the Audit does involve quite a few sums where you add up the minutes you spend on any given task. Please don't feel daunted by any of this. Most people love filling in the charts – they get quite hooked on it. That said, you don't have to complete every single one in order to get a lot out of the Life Audit process. Simply thinking things through can produce amazing changes.

The Life Audit is divided into three stages. The first stage contains a series of charts, spreadsheets and statements. There are some worked examples of the different types of charts for guidance but these are in no way prescriptive. Filling in the charts will enable you to get a complete picture of your life in all its aspects. You'll be learning to listen to those inner voices that tell you what you truly think, and each section includes questions to prompt those thoughts. The first stage will conclude with the Stocktake, which will touch every aspect of your day-to-day living. So, to recap:

FIRST STAGE

This stage establishes who you really are by looking closely at how you spend your time, with whom and doing what, where, when. You will examine how you really feel about the things, events and people you are involved with. Timesheets, questionnaires and analysis will help you find the answers.

By the time you reach the second stage your life will have already shifted – for the better! The task in stage two is to establish a Breakeven position in every area. It will be a survival kit for everything, from your clothes and your health and fitness regime to the housework and home maintenance that needs to be done and the friends and family commitments you have. In this stage you'll be asked lots of questions which are aimed at making you decide on the *minimum* energy and time you are prepared to commit to any given part of your life. This will enable you to come up with that Breakeven expenditure.

You'll be cutting the deadwood out of your life in terms of actions, events and people. Plus there are loads of timesaving tips to enable you to crank extra time out of your schedule while leaving your 'must-do' priorities catered for and identifying areas that have the capacity for change and growth.

Even if you don't move beyond that stage in the Life Audit you will already have achieved a lot. You will have a calm and fulfilled life with obligations, responsibilities and the niceties taken care of, and you will be able to sleep easy at night. Quick recap:

SECOND STAGE

This is all about prioritising and eliminating. You will establish the Breakeven position in all aspects of your life. From the information gathered in the first stage you will be able to clarify what time you need to devote to obligations, responsibilities and relationships. Timesaving advice will help you add value to the hours of each day.

Introduction

17

And what will you be doing with all the spare time you find you have? You'll be getting a life, won't you? Realising those dreams, being brave, being ambitious, having a go! In stage three you'll be putting your plans, dreams and ambitions in place.

By the time you've reached the end of this book you won't be sitting there thinking and wishing, or wondering and fearful. You'll be living big-time! You'll have put your house in order and got your priorities right, and you'll be doing the best by yourself that you can. In fact, you'll be able to get the very best out of the life you've got.

THE
life ⏱
audit

first
stage

Filling in Your Life Audit –
who are you?

Now you are ready to begin filling in your own Audit. My belief that each of us holds the answers to our own life's dilemmas and decisions is only true if we can learn how to read our innermost feelings and be absolutely honest with and about ourselves. For you to do that successfully, you need to be very clear about the person you are.

So you are eagerly poised to begin the journey – but here's a spanner in the works straight off. It's highly likely that the person you *think* you are isn't the person you actually are at all. How do I know? By making so many discoveries about myself, and by hearing about those that others have made about themselves. Our personalities and thought processes are like a set of clothes that we put on day in and day out, and frankly don't particularly notice any more. We don't see the colour, the light and shade, the texture or the weave of the fabric, and we may also have stopped noticing the actual cut or fit.

Even if you are very clear-cut about yourself and what you want to achieve by carrying out this Audit of your life, I expect you will uncover some surprising revelations about the person you really are. And if your starting point is one of uncertainty or even boredom about what the future holds, then the Life Audit will add clarity and focus to the dreams and ambitions you don't even know you hold at the moment.

The Life Audit starts by asking you to come up with some simple statements and assumptions in two personal statements. As you proceed through the first stage of the process, you will keep making discoveries about yourself that will change your self-perception. It's going to be rather like getting better acquainted with a person you've met in passing and, in so doing, discovering layers of interests and opinions that weren't immediately obvious.

You'll need to get into the mindset of acknowledging what these things reveal about yourself. Be kind to yourself; if you unveil some unpleasant characteristics or aspects of your life, acknowledge them and adjust the picture of yourself accordingly. For instance, I had to face up to the fact that deep down I'm lazy. I grasped this pretty quickly when, having created the free time to take more exercise, get on top of the housework and learn to play golf, I then really had to galvanise myself and stop finding other excuses.

Tom understood within a couple of days of auditing how much he avoided dealing with issues that caused him grief. 'I was forever putting off sorting out problems – so much so that they would start out as molehills and become mountains. It nearly always involved having to have a frank chat with someone – a colleague, my wife or daughter – about something I was concerned about. I watched myself avoiding situations and finding reasons not to have these confrontations, and then saw the situations getting worse by the minute.'

Jane said she felt embarrassed when her Audit showed up her mania for housework. 'I wrote on my wish list that I wanted to meet more people, get a boyfriend and have more fun, so what on earth was I doing spending most of the weekend tidying an already tidy home and not going out anywhere?'

Sarah was shocked at how resistant she was to freeing up some time. 'I couldn't seem to prioritise at all, and watched myself finding things to do and virtually making the kids need me to be in Mummy or Granny mode all the time.' Gillian was the same. 'I had a list of things I wanted to do but I was reluctant to give up being needed by others, and even though I moan about it all the time I heard myself asking my daughter-in-law which nights she wanted me to pick up my grandsons from school and make their teas.'

So be prepared to find some aspects of doing the Life Audit embarrassing or shaming. Some professional therapists say you have to learn to love yourself before you can 'grow'. I think you also need to face up to any personal 'bad behaviour' and probably address it, because it's likely to be having an adverse affect on your life or on others. However, by the same token enjoy gathering the evidence that reinforces your good points and that makes you lovable or enhances your life. It's so important that you get to know yourself thoroughly and that you are ultra-honest with yourself.

But before all that, the first question you must address is how private are you going to be able to keep your notes. It's going to be hard enough at times being honest with *yourself* about some aspects of your life, let alone writing things down that may fall into the wrong hands. Remember, you may be writing down the names of friends you plan to drop, bad personal habits you want to break, your innermost wants and desires, or health worries you'd only care to share with your doctor. You should consider the impact of telling partners, family or close acquaintances about doing the Audit. Obviously there will be curiosity and, if there are any negative entries about them, the potential for domestic drama. However, the experience of most Life Auditors indicates that doing the Audit becomes a talking point, a forum for discussion

The Life Audit

22

about the things that matter in life generally and communally, even though you are essentially doing it for yourself.

Now you are ready to begin – but first, a quick word about chart-filling. By necessity you need to keep account of what happens in your life each day. That means writing it down, and if the thought of that seems daunting be reassured by the experience of others that it quickly becomes an addictive process. You can put as little or as much time as you want into the process, and you can make the notes as brief or as detailed as you need to reach the informed conclusions you are aiming for. Even one-word prompts might suffice. Some of the charts may not seem relevant to your life and you may choose not to fill them in at the moment. Remember, though, that the more data you collect the more information you have to work with and the more surprising the discoveries you may make. Pencils poised, then? Let's go!

Personal Information – facts and figures

The first thing you need to do is to fill in the two sheets that provide a kind of personal 'situation report' for the here and now before you start deciding on any changes you want to make to your life. The first of these, the Personal Information page, can say as much or as little about you as you wish. It's an opening statement of fact about *who* you are, *what* you are, *where* you live, *with* whom and doing *what*. It's all straightforward information, which makes it a pragmatic starting point,

First Stage

the sort of information you would put down on an application form although maybe rather more wide-ranging and more concerned with the minutiae. When I began my Life Audit I was overwhelmed by what I saw as a sprawling and chaotic life that needed such a radical overhaul that I couldn't see where to start. Stating the proverbial obvious seemed as good a place as any.

The main function of this page, then, is to get you on your way – you won't need any soul-searching to fill in the boxes, and it will only take a few minutes to do. There is space at the top of the page in which to put a passport-size photo of yourself if you want to. This is an optional extra, and might seem an odd thing to do in a journal that is 'for your eyes only'. But you are, after all, doing this exercise because in a sense you have lost sight of yourself, and on a page that is saying not a lot more than 'this is what you see' a picture seems rather appropriate. The first time I did the Audit I didn't bother to stick in a photo, but when it became a more formal process I did. I found it added a dimension of 'connection' with myself as well as augmenting the process of looking at someone I quickly realised I didn't know as well as I thought I did. Throughout the Audit process I kept going back to the Personal Information pages and I would find myself looking rather quizzically at the picture, with varying degrees of confusion and dawning comprehension of the person in it. Don't tell me you've never talked to your reflection in a mirror while shaving or putting on your make-up – it's that sort of thing. But it's absolutely not compulsory.

At the bottom of the page there is a blank section for adding any further information that is pertinent only to you. Drawing on my experiences and those of others, I've

1 **Personal Information**   *Date*

Me

Height 5'6"

Weight 9 stone 3 pounds

Skin tone Fair

Eye colour Blue

Hair colour Blonde   Length Shoulder

Age 34   Date of birth 21/07/1970

Distinguishing features Small mole on collarbone

Health problems Asthma, migraines

Picture of myself

Family

Marital status Single

Dependants None

Home

Address 86 Albion Road, Peterborough

Tel. 01705 7488618   Mobile 07974 390855

Email Joanne.Smith@yahoo.co.uk

Type of accommodation Own flat

Work

Occupation Legal secretary

Business address Merritt & Jones, 46 Beachside Ave

Tel. 01705 9455166

Email jsmith@m&j.co.uk

Annual income £21,000

Notes

tried to include most areas of life in the questions. But there may well be other issues, facts and statements that comprise a very important component of what makes up *you*, and at each stage and on most charts of the Life Audit there is space for you to add individual data about things unique to you in the statement box.

The worked example here's just to get you started. See chart 1.

Really Personal Information – ambitions and frustrations

Now, just think back to the reasons that prompted you to buy this book, because those will inspire what needs to be written in this section. Presumably the idea of 'auditing' your time grabbed you. Perhaps that's because you have a list of things you long to do but never get around to. Or maybe you are fed up with having to spend time doing things you dislike.

This chart will sort out which parts of your life are worth hanging on to and which need to be minimised, if possible. It also asks you to confront those niggling regrets we all have and, most important of all, to write down your dreams, large and small. See chart 2.

It's a really useful exercise and you'll immediately notice some recurring themes – after all, most regrets have an opposite desire on a wish list. What you have to do is find a way to disperse the sadness of lost opportunities and realise the dreams. Don't exclude anything on the basis of it being too small or too large. If you regret picking that spot that has now left you with an acne scar, write it

If I had more time I would
- Stay in touch with my friends more regularly
- Write my diary more frequently
- Do some voluntary work
- Take regular exercise
-

I resent time spent on
- Personal admin
- Listening to friends' niggles and worries _all_ the time
- Commuting to work
- Dealing with my boss's home life intruding into office time
-

I love spending time on
- My nephews and nieces
- My garden
- Planning trips abroad
- Mark!
-

My regrets
- Not keeping up acting after school
- Never making it to see Auntie Jean before she died
- Not leaving Rob a year earlier than I did
- Not going to South America when I had the chance
-

My wishes
- To go to India on holiday
- To take up tap dancing
- To get on top of personal finances
- To research voluntary work abroad
-

Notes

down. If you wish you could change the world, put it down on paper. If you don't know where to start identifying your feelings about your current life, wishes and regrets, try some self-interrogation.

Ask yourself these questions:

- *What do you do in your day-to-day life that makes you grumpy?*
- *What things in life do you look forward to?*
- *Is there a theme you keep coming back to when depressed about something you regret?*
- *When feeling hopeful and optimistic, do you talk about plans you have for the future?*
- *In terms of a day, a week and a year, what would be your ideal life?*

Keep coming back to this page. You should need at least one supplementary sheet before the process is over. The Life Audit is an investigation into yourself, a luxury that you have never enjoyed before, and with any luck you will be finding out all sorts of things about yourself that you hadn't known before. You may find that some of the things you are writing down at the beginning of this exercise cease to be relevant as you proceed. Don't scrub them out completely. Just draw a line through and come back to them at the end to evaluate what has happened that made them less important than they were when you first wrote them down.

Your Time Spreadsheet – making every minute count

Time to get on now with the serious business of collecting the data you will need to make certain informed decisions about your life. These decisions will help you implement some of those wishes you have just articulated and scale down the irritations of life while dispensing with the regrets.

The minutes of each day are your currency, and it is important that you have a clear idea about where you are spending your time in the present so that you can make adjustments later. You are going to keep a close account of where the minutes go. There are Daily Time Logs for you to fill in, and each day also has a Day Journal and an optional Pie Chart in which you can write down explicit detail and get a visual idea of your time use.

The Life Audit will work for you whether you do it for a week, a month or any period of time in between. Decide now what period you want an overview of, and as you add up your time commitments work them out for that timespan. At the back of the book you will find gridded sheets that represent a day, a week, a month and a year. These are note sheets for rough workings out to give you an overview of your chosen period of time, which all depends on the degree of complexity of your life, your relationships and the decisions you need to make.

I carried out my own Life Audit over a 28-day period because that length of time worked for me. I found it useful to have the discipline of daily timekeeping over that span of time in order to monitor how effective small changes in my routine became. Each day's form-filling took about half an hour, and, given that the plan is to make life-changing decisions, 28 days of book-keeping in this way didn't seem an excessive amount of time to sacrifice. I then worked out the roll-on time implications across a full year because I wanted to get the big picture and see how big Z (Time Available, if you recall) was for long-term plans. But of course the only person you are doing this for is *you*, so you may decide on a different period of time. The Life Audit does not promise to change your life in X number of days. The Life Audit's 'offer' is to help you come up with a bespoke plan and schedule that will help you to make personally informed changes for you, in your own time, related to your own unique life.

You are about to put the minutiae of that life under a magnifying glass. Remember, the more data you enter, the more material you will have to work with. It's equally important that you keep reminding yourself that, certainly at present, it is only for your eyes. This is the beginning of a very personal journey to find out all about *you*.

Hole punch the three sheets for each day of this first stage and put them into your ring binder. If you want to jot down incidental thoughts too, get a small notebook to carry in your pocket or bag.

Daily Time Log

Let's start with the Daily Time Log, which is a very straightforward grid. All 24 hours of each day have to be accounted for. That's 48 half-hours or 96 quarter-hours. There are 24 hours marked down the left-hand side of the grid, and each hour box covers four quarter-hours.

Across the top are blank boxes for you to write down the activities you filled your time with, such as sleeping,

The Life Audit

work, housework, exercise, travelling and so on. The row of boxes at the bottom is for you to total up the time spent by the end of the day on each activity.

These are the most frequently used categories:

- Work
- Domestic
- Personal
- Social
- Travel
- Exercise
- Leisure
- Hobbies
- Shopping
- Sleep

Think carefully about the life activities you are describing before labelling them. Where two categories collide, such as exercise and leisure, try to be honest with yourself about the dominant reason for doing the activity. Are you playing badminton to stay fit? Or because it's something that makes you relax and therefore qualifies as leisure? Or is it mainly a way of getting together with other people and therefore a social activity? If your categories aren't clear-cut, spend a couple of days trying to define them before you start your plan. And do remember that you must be careful to avoid 'double accounting'. Time only counts once, which is why it's crucial that you're honest about which category an activity falls into.

Remember, too, that the categories you put at the top of the grid are inclusive, not exclusive, so you need to give additional information in the notes section on the far right. For instance I put 'domestics' in my top box when I am talking about cleaning, washing, loading the dishwasher, ironing and so on, and in my side box I noted the specific chore I was doing at the time.

Here you can write down all manner of things as your day progresses, such as who you spent time with, what

Daily Time Log

Date _____ Day _____

a.m.	Sleep	Work	Travel	Leisure	Exercise	Domestic	Relationships	Notes
1	x							
2	x							
3	x							
4	x							
5	x							
6	x							Good night's sleep, pottered round house
7	x					x		Commute to work, reading
8			x			x		
9		x	x					
10		x						Having a coffee break, Adam popped into my head - must get in touch
11		x						
12		x						Lunch meeting, missed having a break
13		x						
14		x						Had to run to bank – I really need to sort out online banking!
15		x			x			
16		x						
17		x		x				Quick trip to the gym
18			x	x				Travel to Mark's – took ages, arrived late
19			x					Lovely evening once I'd relaxed
20							x	
21							x	
22							x	
23	x						x	
24	x						x	
Totals	8	8.25	2	1	1	1.25	3.5	**Totals** 24

you wore and what you ate. The notes section will become increasingly important, not only to record the details of your time use but also, as you learn to read your feelings, as a place to record the pluses and minuses of daily activities. You'll be surprised at the random thoughts, emotions and memories you'll suddenly start registering. It's rather like training a *Big Brother* camera on yourself – even such banalities as scratching your nose shouldn't go unnoticed. (Joke! Well, maybe not. A persistently itchy nose might need cross-referencing later under Health.)

In the example I've used crosses to mark off the time – some people prefer ticks. In this and many other respects it's up to you to customise these pages to suit you and your way of life.

At the end of each day you need to add up the amount of time you spent doing things and enter it in the appropriate box at the bottom. Be prepared to be surprised! Double-check your addition by making sure the total time comes to 24 hours.

FILLING IN YOUR DAILY TIME LOG

- *See chart 3.*
- *Enter 'sleep' in the first top box and cross off the number of hours since midnight that you have been asleep.*
- *If you went to bed after midnight, make that activity your first entry.*
- *Select inclusive umbrella headings that encompass the day's activities.*
- *As your day progresses, continue to enter general activity headings along the top and to mark the time*

First Stage

they take, working down the hours of the day listed on the left-hand side.

- *Make supplementary notes on the right-hand side to explain the detail and breakdown of the activity. Use one-word prompts if appropriate.*
- *Remember to record thoughts and emotions.*
- *Fine-account to the nearest quarter-hour if you want.*
- *Be very careful not to double account.*
- *At the end of the day, add up the time spent on each category.*
- *Work in decimal, i.e. 1.25, 0.5, 2 and so on – it makes the maths easier.*
- *Make sure the total adds up to 24.*

Pie Charts

You can create a graphic visualisation of your day through the Pie Charts, which are optional but very effective. Simply translate the various portions of your day on to the top chart. Use different types of cross-hatching, or coloured pencils if you have any to hand. You will see as you are shading in the sections where the balance of your day is right and where you have got it wrong. You will know better than anyone where the wasted minutes are on that segmented circle that represents 24 hours of your life.

Remember those regrets, dreams, hopes and fears you wrote down at the beginning of the Audit? Looking at the graphic representation of your day you can ask yourself whether you reinforced any of the negatives or realised any of the positives you wrote down in your Really

Personal Information. Have you managed to do any constructive planning, or moved any of your ideas forward a little? Were you a participant in your life today, or merely a passive spectator as the minutes ticked by?

In the early days of doing the Life Audit you may feel your life is in such a muddle that it is going to be impossible to obtain any sort of clarity. Don't despair – first, the discipline of doing it will prompt you to start eliminating non-essentials and you will find yourself becoming more focused. Second, in the next stage there's lots of guidance from people who've already carried out their Life Audit: they will help you address the different parts of your life to get back to basics and find your ultimate Breakeven position. Very soon you will be looking at that Pie Chart with a critical eye, identifying times of the day that could have been better used. That's where the second Pie Chart comes in – it's for you to redraw your day. With the benefit of hindsight, how *should* the day have gone?

On your first day, your best shot is likely to be a bit of fantasy and no, don't give over a great chunk of time to 'lying in bed eating chocolate and watching soaps'. Taking into consideration what *had* to be done, such as getting the kids off to school, work, football practice, de-fleaing the cat and so on, scrutinise the waking hours you had left and, mindful of all those plans and ambitions you wrote down, but also mindful of how you now feel at the end of the day, rewrite your day's history and then take a long, hard look at it.

Ask yourself these questions:

- *Which areas of your day were devoted to compulsory commitments?*

- *Where did you waste time?*
- *Did you start the day with a plan that you failed to realise?*
- *Did you invest any time today in anything on your wish list?*
- *What could you have done that would have given you a sense of achievement?*

Julia, a 26-year-old recruitment consultant, described this as a bitter-sweet experience. 'The comparison between what I *had* done with my day and what I *wished* I'd done with my day was awful. It was good in that it proved to me that I could take firmer control of how I spent my time. It really showed up how I wasted hours not really doing anything, such as wandering around the shops at lunchtime every day. Then in the evening either seeing the same mates every night or just watching whatever was on the telly.'

Leroy, a 46-year-old hairdresser, found filling in the Pie Chart the most immediately challenging part of the Audit. 'It became a personal campaign each day to make the two charts work out as similar as possible. In fact I drew the second one first thing in the morning and then made myself try and match those good intentions.'

Starting the Audit may feel rather like going on a diet, or reverting to being a child and having the sulks about an enforced chore. What's kept many people going, though, is the stark realisation that if they gave up they'd have to live with themselves and the knowledge that they were making a conscious decision not to rein in the chaos in their life. No one but them would know, but they were their own toughest judges.

What happened

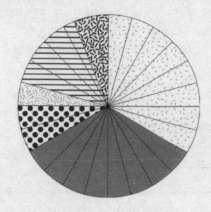

Key

 sleep

work

 travel

 domestic

relationships

 exercise

leisure

What should have happened

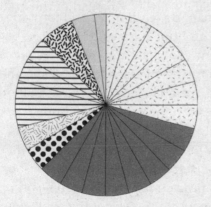

Summary

If I'd got out of bed a bit earlier, I could have had some time in the garden – a bit of leisure time! Would have been great to spend less time travelling, too.

Day Journal

The third chart you need to fill in each day is the Day Journal. Before you groan, do recall that I said form-filling took me less than half an hour a day, and I promise that pretty soon you will find it a quick and instinctive process. As well as helping you further along your Life Audit, the Day Journal acts as a thermometer on how you *feel* about your daily life, starting with the very first question it asks you to address: 'How do you feel about the day ahead?'

Let's assume it's Day One. You are waking up on what you have promised yourself is the first day of the rest of your life because from now on *you* are going to be properly taking charge of what you do. You've got the book, you've read the sections that tell you how to start conducting your Audit and you're lying in bed on the first morning, shrugging off sleep.

The very first 'Audit' action you must do is lie there for

The Life Audit

a few seconds longer and think! You should be excited at the prospect of starting the Life Audit, but momentarily put all thoughts about the process to one side and instead think properly about the day ahead. Gauge your waking thoughts and feelings.

Ask yourself these questions:

- *How did you sleep?*
- *Do you feel physically relaxed and rested?*
- *What's your first thought about the day ahead?*
- *What does it hold?*
- *Do you have a clear emotional response to anything in the coming waking hours?*

And if you can't sense any emotional response to anything? Try harder. Mentally walk yourself through the events and chores that you know are going to occupy your time today. In your mind's eye get up, then travel to work, college or playgroup, have lunch with friends, go to sports practice, do the shopping, come home, make supper and so on. Look at yourself methodically going through the day and think whether the prospect of anything you have just mentally clocked fills you with either delight or misery.

Ask yourself these questions:

- *Do you feel bored?*
- *Do you feel apathetic?*
- *Do you feel exhausted at just the thought?*
- *Do you feel happy?*
- *Do you feel excited?*

Lie still and really *feel* the signals your body and mind are sending out as your subconscious registers what's on the agenda for the day and begins preparing you to face it. It might be a tiny knot in your stomach, a dull yawn being stifled, a delicious warm glow dawning or a faint but urgent drumbeat in your temple heralding what you know lies in store for you today.

Because most of us blunder into the day to get on with our duties and commitments it may not be as easy as you think to be so inwardly reflective, especially first thing in the morning. But remember, this first statement is not asking you to resolve anything or to make it better – you are just taking a small chunk of time to consider yourself and your life. You'll be doing a lot of that over the coming days: trust me when I say you will become increasingly skilled at it as the month progresses.

It was doing this exercise that led to me realising I was bored with my job and ultimately giving it up. When, therefore, I found myself without a 'proper' job to go to every morning, I carried out another Life Audit because I didn't find myself as full of focus as I had expected. The result was equally surprising, and it took me a while to work out my feelings about the day ahead. Here's the thought process:

'As I sit here in bed on the first day of my Life Audit I am aware that my day holds lots of what I call "grunt" work to do – accounts, administration and sorting out. I know too that I must begin, and make progress on, some new work projects. I feel a bit daunted and depressed by that, which on closer examination is because I have doubts in my own ability to get on with things and am already dreading the feeling of non-achievement I may experience at the end of the day. So that's a bit defeatist, isn't it? "Apprehensive" is the word that sums up how I feel, and lacking in a sense of self-confidence or commitment.'

So 'apprehensiveness' was the emotion I finally realised was the over-riding feeling I had about the day ahead, and it worked back to a lack of confidence in my ability to achieve my goals.

Ask yourself a similar question at the end of the day – it will be interesting to see how well or how badly the two responses match. Learning to listen to your inner voices takes practice, and you may make a few false starts. If you come up against a blank non-feeling, however hard you try to 'sense' what you really want or know to be right, try hitting upon one option and spotting the knee-jerk first response to the fact that *that* is the course of action you have decided upon. More often than not you'll have opted for the one that seemed obvious, inevitable or more desirable when in fact it was the one that deep down you knew was not right or true.

The more focused you are on satisfying other people's criteria, needs and opinions, the harder it may be to loosen up and listen to yourself. You are probably very good at being and doing what everyone else wants, or at least what you think is expected of you by others. But just like a relationship with anyone else, the more attention you pay to that real person talking inside you the more you'll get to understand them and hear what they are really saying.

At this moment remember too that you are only *listening*, not *doing*, and you are bound to mishear or misjudge sometimes. That's OK – you shouldn't be taking drastic actions or making 'big' decisions until the end of the Audit process. Give this new relationship with 'you' time to develop until your 'reading' of yourself is more instinctive. At that point you'll feel safer trusting the messages you are getting.

Another part of the Day Journal deserves special mention. At the end of the day you need to think back to the moments that either caused you the most grief or gave you the greatest joy.

At first the extent of my 'blessings counted' was as simple as noticing it was a lovely day. But then, as I became more attuned to picking up on what I really felt, I found myself being cheered by lots of other things, big, small, sometimes very mundane and often completely unconnected to myself. There was the day I was having a business lunch in a London restaurant when on the next table a young couple's baby started to squall. They tried to shush the child while finishing their lunch quickly. The other diners, including me, grimaced at the racket and shared a collective sympathy with the parents. Then a waiter had a quiet word with the mother, took the baby from her, balanced the child on one hip and took his place at the booking desk to meet and greet customers while the maître d' took over his waiting duties. The baby became silent, and was as entranced as the arriving and departing diners were bemused.

It was a simple act of less than earth-shattering importance, but it was also a really life-enhancing moment. As such it affected me – it made me feel happier, kindlier disposed to my fellow humans, and cheered that one stranger had helped another.

Sue said counting her blessings instantly changed the beginning of every day. 'I used to moan about the journey into work and the traffic jam. Then I started noticing some children on their way to school at the same time, and they were so happy and cheerful I started to consciously look out for them each morning. Seeing them cheered me up, transformed the way I felt about the journey and started the day off on a good note. It made a difference.'

Other people who have audited their lives have listed feeding the birds in their garden, watching their grandchildren playing, getting a seat on the bus to work, other drivers' road courtesy, sitting in their garden, afternoon tea, favourite television programmes, reading the papers over a relaxed breakfast, hearing a special piece of music on the radio, time with a close friend and, over and over again, the politeness or kindness of strangers. The reverse was true as well, of course, and it was often small acts of unkindness that provided the worst of the 'miserable moments'. The point is not to underestimate how often really little things – the minor irritations and the simple pleasures – make the biggest impact on your day.

The rest of the Day Journal is straightforward and simply asks you to fill in various items of information. The different categories stem from the issues that I and others who have done the Life Audit wanted to address, and the routines we followed. Adapt it to suit yourself, and use the blank section at the bottom if there is something in your life that is not listed but that you want to keep tabs on. This section has been used for all sorts of things ranging from the number of times you play Solitaire at work when the boss isn't looking to how many packets of wine gums you consume a day. (Bridget Jones would have used it to count the number of lottery instants she bought!)

This Day Journal will be a simplified reference that you will be able to use when doing the reckoning as your Audit

First Stage

Day Journal   *Date*   *Day*   5

I woke up today feeling   *excited and apprehensive*   **about the day ahead**
because   *I'm seeing Mark later but I have a tricky day at work first*

Health

Health issues   *Slight toothache, hay fever* Weight *9 stones 4 pounds*
Exercise   *20 min walk to station x2, hour in the gym*
Supplements   —

Food

Breakfast *Cup of tea, cornflakes*   Beverages *Coffee x 2 with milk*
Lunch *Chicken sandwich, diet Coke*   Alcohol *3 glasses wine*
Supper *Salmon pasta, green salad*   Cigarettes *2*
Snacks *Apple, dried apricots*   Diet units —

Relationship – I spent time today with:

Special person *Mark*   Friends *Sarah & Jenny*
Family *Richard*   Work colleagues *Alex, Alan*
Aquaintances *Dawn*   Support/professional —

Domestic chores   *Washing up, trip to bank to pay cheques in*

Work

Achievements *Didn't put the big job off – felt better for tackling it*
Frustrations *Email still not working properly*

Money

Earned *£80.76*   Spent *£19.58 – lunch, bottle of wine, bus ticket, moisturiser*

Clothes *Matching underwear (!), t-shirt, skirt, sandals, denim jacket, green handbag*
Leisure *Reading a book on train to work, drinks in pub, chat with Mark*
Citizenship *Helped neighbour with pram on to train, signed up to donate to Oxfam*
Miserable moments *Row with Richard. Anxious after. Reading newspaper on bus – world is nasty place*
Blessings counted *Sunny day, have great relationship with brother really*

> Other
>
> *Mostly a really good day – things calming down at work and despite brief row with brother, am lucky to have him. Things going really well with Mark, I think*

I went to bed feeling   *generally positive but a bit worn out*   **about the day**
because   *work went better than expected, everything good with Mark*

progresses. When you write it up is entirely up to you, and there seems to be no 'best' time. I did mine in bed at the beginning and end of each day. Others do it on the Tube, during their lunch hour or while they are watching TV. As long as you are keeping your Time Log through the day, it will be simply a question of referring back to that.

Remember, the more you fill in the more you will get out of the whole process. Much of the data you record here will enable you to fill in accurately the separate Stocktakes, coming up soon, on individual life areas such as home and relationships. The Day Journal gives you the opportunity to account for everything from your innermost feelings to the clothes you wear and the money you spend.

FILLING IN YOUR DAY JOURNAL

- *See chart 5.*
- *Enter the date and number each day of the Audit.*
- *Take time to note how you feel about the day ahead.*
- *Enter relevant details concerning your health, weight and exercise.*
- *Keep your food diary even if you don't have a diet or weight problem.*
- *Note down everyone with whom you have any exchange, including chance encounters with strangers. 'Support/professional' refers to people like your cleaner or nanny, who support you, and your doctor/dentist with whom you have a purely professional relationship.*
- *'Domestic chores' is for writing down the household*

---

chores you do, errands you run, etc.

- Just make a general statement about your working day's achievements and frustrations unless there were specific events or people that provoked a particular good or bad experience.
- 'Work' is a broad term to include study, keeping house or looking after children, duties taken on in retirement and job-hunting if unemployed.
- Whether you are in paid work or receiving benefits, calculate each day's 'earnings' – even if it's just an average or approximation. Enter this figure and the amount of money you spent, giving as much detail as you want. Don't forget there is nothing wrong with using supplementary sheets, one of the worksheets or creating your own bespoke form if you want to keep track of something.
- List all the clothes you wore, including jewellery and accessories.
- 'Leisure' should include anything you do for the sheer pleasure and relaxation it gives you.
- 'Citizenship' is any act, small or large, that touches people's lives outside your own or contributes towards making the world a better place.
- Don't ignore the smallest miserable moment or blessing you can count.
- Take time at the end of the day to identify your over-riding feeling about that day.
- Remember, the more information you can enter on the Day Journal the easier you will find collating data for the Stocktakes.

Don't be terminally discouraged if at first you struggle to find the time to devote to filling in the charts that will enable you to carry out your Life Audit properly. Try to pull together as much information as you can recall, and if in your heart of hearts you know it's only a sketchy representation of the day's events, rub it all out. Likewise, if you miss more than a couple of days in a row it's better to start the whole process again. The idea is to get a picture across a consecutive period of time. If you set yourself a four-week timescale and keep failing when trying to fill in the Daily Time Logs across the month, opt for a week instead and take it seven days at a time.

There's quite a lot of work involved and I've already warned that at times it won't be easy. But, just as with office work or domestic paperwork which, done properly, smooth the path of our daily lives, consider the demanding bits as an investment in the quality of the rest of your life. And be assured that, by the end of the period, you will have built up a detailed and accurate picture of your life and all that touches it.

A reminder about accuracy: no matter how honest you think you are being with yourself, I can guarantee you will find yourself guilty of at least one area of self-delusion – we all do. So can I reiterate that all this data is for your eyes only unless you *choose* to share it with someone else. So only you know how accurate you are being with the information you are recording.

When you've finished, while you'll possibly be glad it's over, trust me that you'll be even more glad you've done it! Good luck!

Your Time Balance Sheet – adding value and making investments

So you are on your way – dutifully filling in your daily sheets and, I hope, by now finding it addictive and not a chore. Also you will quickly realise there is more to it than ticking a few boxes and counting up the hours. The process should start feeling like a gentle rediscovery of yourself – rather like blowing the dust of daily detritus away on the current you and finding the real you underneath.

You may at first go into a state of denial about the things you are revealing about yourself. That will be when you start kidding yourself on the page. Will you or won't you admit that for the second day in a row you ate a whole packet of cheesy strings *and* a pork pie on the way home from the supermarket . . . before supper? Will you be honest enough to note down the irrational irritation you felt when your nearest and dearest kept clearing their throat while watching TV – again! No, you might not be truthful, because you will feel such a heel at being a lesser person than the lovely Life Audit-seeking soul you know you are inside. But you must! Otherwise the whole thing is a nonsense.

However, all is not as bad as it seems. If the month ahead loomed as a painfully humiliating routine of simply chronicling the negatives, even if they were interspersed with happy moments and positive emotions, it would be a pretty destructive process. Most of us don't need to be told our failings more than once, let alone write them down day in day out for a month; we know them already, and we only need so much telling. So once the Life Audit has done its job of flagging up those failings you can start dealing with them, because although the Daily Time Log, Pie Charts and Day Journal are all about collecting information across a considerable timespan, that doesn't mean that you can't and won't start making changes from Day One. Bad habits are as good a starting place as any for the elimination process to begin, although in fact you'll probably be keen to make changes in other areas too – health, home, relationships and leisure, for instance.

So, as you fill in your daily details, start breaking up your life into sectors. You'll be doing that already with the headings you are giving your daily routines at the top of the Daily Time Logs. As you progress through the Audit you'll need to put your life sections through a series of procedures and tests. These have two purposes: first, to calculate any time need they have across a given period, and second, to provide a situation report on the place each section has in your life and your attitude towards it. For example, your fitness level in regard to your health may only need a time allowance if you go to the gym, play a sport or take other specific time out for exercise. The same applies to what I call your 'soul': there may be no time implication at all, unless you devote special time to prayer, meditation or worship. These Stocktakes will also help you eliminate and select what you need to dump and what you need to keep and nurture.

I've chosen the following life 'sectors' to track through the process because they applied to me and to others who have carried out the Life Audit: health, relationships, home, image, money, work, leisure, citizenship, soul and mortality. They are all explained in detail in the next section. The 'tracking' gets going as soon as you begin your Audit process. This is when you start to get 'real' about things – for instance, to regret or resent time spent doing something, or with someone. So it's right and proper that during the process you will start trying to adjust your day to something that is better balanced and a happier experience.

You may decide that some of the sectors are not applicable to your life or the issues you want to deal with, and of course you don't need to fill in all of them. However, the information these charts supply is very important for the success of your Life Audit. You must know what you are looking for and spot where you do begin to make adjustments, so that the final picture is accurate. This is because in the second stage of the Life Audit you will be making bigger decisions that impact heavily on your life, and you shouldn't do that until you have established the true overall picture. If it was possible to do that in one day you wouldn't need to carry out the continuing balance assessment I'm explaining here. But of course a single day's accounting would not prompt the subtle shifts and changes, the added value and investments that you will inevitably achieve over a decent length of time.

In the first place these changes will consist of everyday improvements – simple things like oiling a door hinge to stop it sticking, or making sure your favourite mug is out of the dishwasher first thing in the morning. Even at this mundane level you are adding value to the hours of your day, and you'll get more ambitious as you progress – so much so that you'll be keen to move on to the second stage.

Unless you are really confident that you have achieved the total overview you are aiming for don't leap ahead, because this stage of the Audit is really essential groundwork for making the right decisions later on. It's a time investment in your future and an opportunity to do more than just bring order into your life. In the next stage you will start 'doing' and effecting the changes you need to make to realise some of those items on your wish list. Right now you need to use this reflective stage to double-check that you genuinely do know what you want. So look upon the spare capacity you may be freeing up as an investment in forward planning, and really 'think' about what will improve and enhance your life – both day to day and in the bigger picture.

You will start to notice changes in your attitude almost immediately, but it may not necessarily be all plain sailing. You must have had some level of dissatisfaction with your life to have decided to embark on the Audit in the first place, and you may well discover that some of the findings from your close scrutiny reinforce that sense of discontent.

Geraldine, a 54-year-old teacher, spoke of feeling quite desperate on Day Four as she began to see how one-dimensional her life was. 'It was even "sadder" than I'd thought,' she said. 'Every day the same routines, the same people, the same lack of variety.' At one point in that first week she found doing the daily grids so depressing that she nearly gave up. Luckily she didn't, and in the absence of any good ideas or motivation to 'add value' to her daily routine concentrated instead on the practical aspects of eliminating those habits and happenings that didn't have a positive bearing on her life. She cleared out her cupboards of old clothes, caught up with her personal paperwork and housework, and aimed for a really precise Stocktake.

But Geraldine would be the first to say it wasn't all straightforward. She confessed she felt quite frightened that she was exposing the poverty of her life without any guarantee that she would find better experiences or opportunities to pursue. She even found herself getting panicky about her lack of wishes and of a sense of optimism about her future. Also, of course, at the same time as worrying about that she was also painfully aware that she was undertaking a process designed to leave great swathes of time waiting to be filled – but with what? Geraldine had to have faith that something would occur. 'In a way, I felt completely exposed by my findings,' she said. 'At least my days were full before, and although I didn't have the most exciting of lives I don't think I was actually unhappy. Suddenly, though, I was looking at that life and finding it wanting.'

But there's the clue. Who or what was Geraldine measuring herself against? Whose expectation was she trying to match? The Audit can't apologise for making you confront aspects of your life about which you are in some kind of denial, Remember, no one can *make* you be honest with yourself, and in the same way no one will judge you if you abandon the procedure. But don't give in to discouragement too soon.

Geraldine's problem was that she doubted her own ability to make her life better. While embarking on the Audit because she had a nagging dissatisfaction with her life, she had a struggle relinquishing the passive safety of not confronting those issues and felt she lacked the inspiration to see how things could be made better. Yet recognising her weaknesses was precisely why the idea of the Audit appealed to her. The Audit is all about proactively helping you to confront your timidity, apathy and unhappiness. It's about helping you to take life by the horns and to 'make' it happier, fuller, richer – to do *something* to change circumstances or situations that don't enrich your days. The tiniest of shifts in your daily patterns or attitudes can make everything else move slightly, and so allow 'new' things to come in.

Of course it's easier *not* to do something about an OK life – all you have to do is to put this book down. But for goodness sake, if you are like Geraldine give yourself a break. You are a bright and intelligent person who has decided to be honest about *you*. At least give yourself and life itself a chance to come up with something that will make this scary frankness worthwhile. The Audit will give you all the tools to make life better.

In the end Geraldine did find she had a considerable amount of time on her hands and decided to explore the possibility of turning her cross-stitch hobby into a business. She's set herself the task of assessing the trade at local craft shops and craft markets to see what opportunities there might be to design and sell embroidery kits. She's been to see her bank manager about the assistance available for small businesses and has enrolled on a computer course.

'It's something I could do if I took early retirement and could start preparing for now,' she said. 'I could start small and build it up. But I want to make sure I've done all my research first, and it's great to feel more in control of something I could end up doing in the future.'

'I didn't have much faith in being able to sort out what I knew was my big issue,' said Liz, a 35-year-old accountant. 'I want a baby desperately, but I can't seem to find someone to have a really good relationship with and I'm terrified that time will run out. My whole life seems to

First Stage

revolve around that central thing.'

Liz did find a way to deal with this over-riding pressure. First, she decided to look into the possibility of having some of her eggs harvested. Then she entered into a loving pact with a single close male friend that he would father a baby for her if they were both still single when she reached forty. And finally she is looking into the possibility of being considered as a single foster parent. 'Now I feel I can get back on with living, and that every meeting with a man is not the beginning of a race against time to fall in love and get married.' In this way Liz was able to take the pressure off today by addressing the fears she had about the future.

Before you can start planning for your own future, though, you need to make sure you've done all your research into your current life. The data you have gathered over the time you have been looking closely at your life is the material that will furnish you with the information you need to make important decisions further down the Audit process. Just being honest with yourself is adding value and making an investment in the hours and days that make up your unique life.

Stocktake Your Life – daily logs and double entries

Time and the way you use it is the currency of the Audit, but the other checks and controls will bring clarity and focus into the rest of your life. Keeping your Daily Time Log will show you how you spend your time and also how much time in your life is surplus to basic requirements. The Audit may throw up some contradictions in your life. In one area, such as your home or relationships, you may need to set about a process of elimination, cutting out the deadwood and chaff. In other areas you may, just like Geraldine, spot some gaping voids.

With the Time Logs chronicling your time use, the purpose of the Stocktakes is to try to define everything that is in 'daily use', that you spend time on and that is important to you – everything from friends, to clothes to your thoughts on your mortality. A Stocktake will help you come up with a stock control level that will allow you to function at an optimum level. No waste, nothing perishing, nothing gathering dust. This stock control level is your Breakeven position reached as a result of scrutinising your life over the time period of the Audit.

At its most basic a stocktake is a physical count of all stocks at the end of a financial year. The time you decide to devote to your Audit is your run-up to year-end and will allow you to shed immediately obvious surplus stock. As you move on to the second and third stages of the Audit your parameters will inevitably change, but for now you are aiming to get the most accurate picture possible of your current needs.

The first thing to do is to decide upon the length of your Audit period. That might be a week, a month, or a year. You will be noting down your use of time over this specific period and recording that amount in the totals box.

You will need to do the sum to calculate the total time commitment each activity will require across your total Audit period. So if, for example, your Audit period is one week and you identify something that takes up a quarter of an hour each day, you will need to multiply it by seven to get the total time commitment. If your Audit period was a four-week month you would need to multiply it by 28, and so on. You need to identify, as you are noting down time use, whether the activity is something that happens daily, weekly, monthly or whatever, by simply noting d, w, m or y.

Then you need to mark up your totals box accordingly, having done the necessary multiplication to come up with the total for your Life Audit period, which you are eventually going to transfer to your Time Balance Sheet (chart 25).

Decide whether you intend to work out the bigger picture of your time use across a year. Remember, you have the blank Year Grid at the back of the book (chart 47), which will help you to calculate how many times an incident or event is likely to occur and to take account of different days such as holidays or weekends when your routine may be different. Some sectors will have events that need time devoted to them once or twice a year – unless they actually happen during your Audit period, these only need to be anticipated and recorded if you are going to calculate that bigger 12-month picture.

Once you've gathered all the information about the things, encounters and commitments in your life that need your attention you'll be able to plot the time this basic stock uses each day. Then you'll get a clear view of what time you have left to play with.

The aim for each element of your life is either to assess its time need calculated in hours across a period of time, or to make it a sorted-out ticked box that requires no further consideration.

STOCKTAKE SECTORS

- *Health – wellbeing, fitness, and diet and weight loss*
- *Relationships – partners, family, friends, acquaintances, colleagues, children, pets, professionals and support services*
- *Home – bricks and mortar, contents, housework, maintenance*
- *Image – clothes, grooming, style*
- *Money – income and expenditure, total worth*
- *Work – time value, satisfaction*
- *Leisure – time value, satisfaction*
- *Citizenship – responsibility and concern*
- *Soul – identity and concern*
- *Mortality – attitude and concern*

At the end of some of the Stocktake charts is a space for you to make an auditor's statement that sums up where you are with that particular area of your life. This should be a sentence that defines your headline concerns or state of contentment. What you are trying to obtain is a picture of now and of what importance you attach to the issues you find need addressing.

Health Stocktake

The Audit Stocktake section starts with health because if you aren't functioning well physically it will probably blight everything else. But the concept of health isn't limited to being physically well or ill, of course. We are all very well informed today that the concept of being a

First Stage

57

healthy person must encompass diet and fitness too. This Stocktake of your health will seek to assess your level of fitness and give you an opportunity to address any diet or weight issues.

There are two charts, one on health and one on fitness, for you to fill in with information collected from your Daily Time Log and Day Journal. There is also an optional Diet and Weight Loss chart because so many people who do the Life Audit combine keeping a food diary with starting a diet and trying to lose weight.

Physical wellbeing

Really think about the day-to-day aches and pains and twinges you feel, from headaches to ingrowing toenails. In your Daily Time Log and Day Journal you should be making notes about your health and fitness. The object of the Stocktake is to end up with a clear and matter-of-fact understanding of the condition of your body. You should not be writing a 'need to do' list to reach Olympic fitness. If that's your wish, it should already be on your Really Personal Information and is something you can address later.

Most of us have at least one aspect of our health or fitness that could do with improvement, and this is an area where you will very easily and quick-ly be able to add value, invest in the future and make serious capital from a little forward planning. You need to consider what your expectations are of your body. These will differ widely depending on your stage of life.

Amita, a 52-year-old mother of three, said all she cared about healthwise was that she and her family and friends continued to be as healthy as they could in order to carry on leading the active life they enjoyed. Me too – I just want my body to function adequately, not super-efficiently, and I certainly don't want it to be a temple. This is mainly because I prefer it to be low-maintenance and no bother. I want to know that I am doing whatever I should and can to keep it functioning and 'not ill', and that I'm not storing up any problems for the future. I might of course like it to be a different shape, but that's more to do with vanity. What we are talking here is health, not beauty.

Just as you'll start picking up on your innermost emotional feelings and gut reactions during the Audit, you'll also find yourself 'listening' to the physical messages your body is sending out. Try to track the origin of any ache or pain and see whether something triggered it. Be alert, too, to the physical manifestations of stress and worry. Is it perhaps anxiety that has brought on a headache, prevented you sleeping soundly or made you feel exhausted?

Bob, a 48-year-old salesman, was shocked by the number of times he wrote down in the course of a day that he felt tired. 'Actually I realised that I was even waking up feeling tired having had ten hours' sleep. I went to see the doctor, and he said that being tired all the time (TATT) was a twenty-first century disease. I don't think it's anything to do with physical exhaustion. I have a lot of business-related worries, and I need to get to the bottom of what else in my life is making me feel so worn out.'

Ask yourself these questions:

- *Does anything about your health prevent you or deter you from doing something you want to do?*
- *Do you regularly have days off work due to illness?*
- *Do you have aches and pains that you tend to ignore?*
- *Is there anything you do that triggers a health problem?*

Health Stocktake: Physical Wellbeing

Date

	Problem	Triggers	Impact & Management	Time req'd (d w m y)	Check-up frequency	Time req'd (d w m y)
Arms	–					
Back	Bit stiff in the morning	Saggy old mattress?				
Blood pressure	Definitely fine last year				Annual	0.5 hrs (y)
Bowels	–					
Breasts	–					
Cholesterol	No idea!					
Ears	–					
Eyes	–					
Face	–					
Feet	Painful hard skin	Pointy sandals	Chiropodist	2 hours (y)		
Hair	–					
Hands	Very dry	Cold weather	Apply handcream	5mins (d)		
Head	Occasional migraine	Stress, red wine	4 hours in bed twice a year	8 hours (y)		
Heart	–					
Hips	–					
Intimate	–				Annual	1 hr (y)
Kidney	–					
Legs	–					
Liver	Feels heavy, achey	Drinking alcohol	–			
Lungs	Asthma	Pollution, smoking	Order & pick up repeat prescription	1 hour (m)	Twice a year	1 hr (y)
Mouth	Cold sores	Stress, tiredness	–			

6.2

	Problem	Triggers	Impact & Management	Time req'd (d w m y)	Check-up frequency	Time req'd (d w m y)
Muscles	–					
Neck	–					
Nose	–					
Skin	–					
Stomach	Bit bloated	Carbs, period				
Teeth	–	–			Annual	0.5 hrs (y)
Throat	–					
Other	Hangovers!	Stress – excessive drinking	Other forms stress relief: yoga	1 hour (w)	–	
	Hay fever	Pollution, pollen		5mins (d)		

Audit period = 28 days

	sub total	x	total (audit period)	x	total (year)
daily (d)	10 mins	x 28	280mins = 4.6hrs	x365	60.8 hrs
weekly (w)	1 hr	x 4	4 hrs	x52	52 hrs
monthly (m)	1 hr	x 1	1 hr	x12	12 hrs
other (y) i.e. yearly, twice yearly	13 hrs				13 hrs
Amount to transfer			9.6 hrs		137.8 hours

Statement

I'm in pretty good shape apart from the occasional migraine which is under control and the ongoing niggles like hay fever and cold sores. Bigger worries are asthma - OK at the minute but don't want to get worse and the odd hangover - too old to recover easily now and not good for stress levels

- *When you wake up do you feel rested, drugged, tense from your dreams?*
- *Are you stiff or are your joints creaky?*
- *When you stretch are you aware of any aches or pains?*
- *How does your tongue look in the bathroom mirror?*
- *What colour is your urine, pale or dark?*
- *Do you feel tired during the day even when you have had plenty of sleep?*
- *Do you sleep badly?*
- *Do you feel irrationally tense or depressed?*
- *Do you reach for a drink or cigarette when under pressure?*
- *Are you stoical about a niggling health problem?*

During this first stage you need to consider each and every moving part of the machine that is your body. You need also to think about regular health checks and routine monitoring and check-ups: are you up-to-date? If you are already diligent about health indicators such as blood pressure or cholesterol note it down on the chart as part of your current health management.

Remember, you aren't looking for specific medical problems. You're aiming for a comprehensive performance report which will equate to the time commitment you need to make for your healthcare and management. This amount will be entered on to the Balance Sheet you will fill in at the beginning of the second stage.

Finally on this chart you will need to come up with an auditor's statement that defines you and your health. Here, as well as providing a summary of your current physical wellbeing, you must account for habits that are likely to affect your health such as smoking, excessive drinking, and drug or painkiller abuse.

FILLING IN YOUR HEALTH STOCKTAKE: PHYSICAL WELLBEING

- *See chart 6.*
- *During the period of your Time Log note down any health problems affecting parts of the body listed on the left of the chart.*
- *Try to concentrate on each body part listed and give a status report on how it feels, noting any ailment in the first column.*
- *The second column asks you to note any trigger circumstances that prompted the problem, such as environmental factors like a high pollen count causing hay fever.*
- *The third column is for you to note the impact it has on you and the kind of steps you need to take to manage it.*
- *Then in the fourth column, note that time consequence. For instance, if you suffer from migraines, do you have to lie down in a darkened room for a couple of hours when you have an attack?*
- *The fifth column is for you to note any necessary check-ups and appointments.*
- *Finally, in the sixth column, record the amount of time they take up.*
- *Calculate the time related to health issues, across the period you plan to assess, and write this into the box on the bottom left to carry forward to the Balance Sheet.*
- *Do remember not to double account.*
- *The statement box is for you to come up with a report on your physical wellbeing, having spent this time considering all aspects of it, good and bad. Treat*

Fitness

The aim of the next chart is to assess your level of fitness – it's a performance report on how active you are and how your body's fitness is maintained. It isn't asking you to match yourself against any particular standard of athleticism or to pit yourself against a fitness fanatic friend (however, if you don't currently do anything that really tests your fitness level you may need to concentrate hard to come up with a true evaluation). The chart also asks you to come up with an auditor's statement about how your level of fitness matches your expectations and your current life demands.

How often do you think about your level of fitness? Every time you go to the gym? Or only when you have to run for the bus or chase after a grandchild? If you are rather shamefaced about your lack of activity, be encouraged by the fact that many Life Auditors find it easy to build more time for fitness into their lives as soon as they get going on the Audit process. But be fair on yourself, and don't forget to take account of your physicality during the day. Vacuuming, weeding the garden, trips to the post room and going up stairs all contribute to movement and mobility.

Different stages of life and different circumstances mean that your fitness level is a variable factor. Although going to the gym is part of many people's lives and can incorporate leisure and social aspects too, for many others their level of fitness is simply a by-product of the general level of activity of their daily lives. The busy mother with three kids and a full-time job may be kept fit by tearing around keeping on top of everything. Later on, however, when her life calms down, will she compensate for the loss of exercise opportunity with something else? Maybe not, and the tendency might be to blame her stiff back or lack of puff just on getting older.

So it's important not to kid yourself about how fit you are in this Stocktake part of the process. Having completed this stage of looking honestly at the way your body functions against the day-to-day tasks you currently set it, later in the Audit you will maybe raise your game to match your fitness to the demands that realising some of your dreams will make.

Remember, the aim is to come up with a situation report on your current level of fitness and how well or poorly it corresponds to the demands you make on your body at the moment. If, like many others, you start to increase your commitment to fitness while clocking how you spend your hours each day, reflect this enthusiasm in your calculations if you are sure you are going to keep it up.

Ask yourself these questions:

- *What do you do that requires you to move around during the day?*
- *How sedentary are you?*
- *Are there specific times when you exercise?*
- *Do you tend to choose activity over inactivity, i.e. do you take the stairs rather than the lift?*
- *Is the effort you put into your fitness an effort? Enjoyable? Imperative?*
- *How often does your fitness level get tested?*

- *Are you aware of any diminishing fitness level?*
- *Does your lifestyle mean you should pay closer attention to fitness?*

The charts for your Fitness Stocktake and analysis simply require you to account for the amount of physical activity you do in any given period of time. A 24-hour grid with a bottom line of inertia and a top line of puffin' sweatin' activity gives you something to measure a day against, and that way you can include washing the car, walking the dog and shopping alongside the workout at the gym. You will be drawing the data from the entries in your Time Logs and Day Journals. Sleep is the ultimate inertia, while a gym workout or game of an energetic sport is optimum activity. Sitting in the car or at your desk is being inactive, while housework, walking around, shopping and similar tasks are active.

Fill in several of these charts across the period of keeping your Time Log. This will ensure that you obtain a true picture of the activity in your day and so can come up with some accurate figures to enter into the time boxes on the bottom left.

FILLING IN YOUR HEALTH STOCKTAKE: FITNESS

- *See chart 7.*
- *Chart your day's level of activity from waking up to going to bed.*
- *Mark the grid with crosses, and then join them up to make a graph.*

Health Stocktake: fitness

Date _____   No. _____

Activities

Activities	1	2	3	4	5	6	7	8	9	10	11	12	13	14	15	16	17	18	19	20	21	22	23	24
Very active																								
i.e. working out Yoga (w)																								
Walk to station (d) (20 mins x 2)									X									X		X	X			
Active																								
Getting up / lunch							X						X											
Travel								X		X									X			X		
Work / at home											X	X	X	X	X	X	X						X	
Inactive																								
sleep	X	X	X	X	X	X																		X
Time	1	2	3	4	5	6	7	8	9	10	11	12	13	14	15	16	17	18	19	20	21	22	23	24

Audit period = 28 days

	sub total	x	total audit period	x	year
daily (d)	40 mins	x 20	800mins = 13.3hrs	x 261	174 hrs
weekly (w)	2 hrs	x 4	8 hrs	x 48	96 hrs
monthly (m)		x 1		x 12	
other (y) i.e. yearly, twice yearly					
Amount to transfer			21.3 hrs.		270 hrs

Statement

I'm a bit complacent about fitness but this really appalled me, and this is a good day with my yoga class! Office job doesn't help, but now I've done this a few times, I need to stop making excuses and build more time in. Maybe a run in the morning sometimes? I can't afford gym membership, especially if I waste the money by not going, so will need to find time to run or swim, as my fitness level is not high enough.

Diet and weight loss

Blame it on the media, blame it on social pressure, blame it on fast food – being overweight is an issue for many people, and it has a direct bearing on health and a strong link with fitness and exercise. Doing the Life Audit may be the time to stop blaming everyone but yourself. This is not a weight loss or diet book – but because there are so many diets out there, each with its fans and fads, the Day Journal offers you space to keep a food diary. Here you can enter the calculated diet unit of choice, be it points, calories, grams of fat or whatever.

You don't need me to tell you that the equation to which you have to find the optimum solution for you is intake of food versus energy expended. If you are a dieter you will probably be well informed already – in fact, with the plethora of books, weight loss plans and media coverage we should all be experts. So it's strange that so many of us fail to lose weight or to stick to a balanced diet. But maybe doing the Life Audit has given you renewed focus and determination.

I was a complete diet junkie, and in the course of my

first Life Audit month did a bit of Weightwatchers, some Atkins and a touch of Rosemary Conley. I must have been pretty confused, but that was how I lived and my weight was an issue for me. As was food – I loved it. If weight is one of your big issues, I can guarantee that having to write a detailed food diary in your Day Journal will be enough to prompt you to start making adjustments to your daily diet which will need to be accounted for accurately throughout the month.

So, whatever unit you are counting in fill in your daily intake, and if you decide to start dieting from Day One, here's a chart specially for you. It sets your weight loss target against the time you are giving yourself to achieve it, and starkly shows up your degree of success. It was motivational for me and really worked, as it has for many others too.

FILLING IN YOUR HEALTH STOCK-TAKE: DIET AND WEIGHT LOSS

- *See chart 8.*
- *It's up to you to choose the units of time to enter along the bottom. Although it's frowned upon by many diet plans, lots of Life Auditors opt to divide the chart up day by day and use a daily weigh-in. Do whatever works for you.*
- *The vertical line is for weight units, and again you can choose whether it's lb or kg.*
- *Finally, make a statement that defines you and your attitude to your weight if it's something you're concerned about.*

Once you have completed all the charts to do with your health and fitness you will be in an informed position to come up with a personalised game plan in the second stage of the Life Audit. This will put you in the best possible condition for the life you want to lead.

Relationship Stocktake

More curiosity and interest have been shown in how one audits one's relationships than in any other area of the plan. In a way, looking at the people I spent my time with when my husband and sons were suddenly away from home all week was my starting point for creating the Life Audit. You are now going to carry out a Stocktake on all your relationships, from those with your partner and closest friends to those with passing acquaintances and people who make up your domestic or professional support services.

There are three documents for you to fill in. The first places on a circular chart in relation to you all the people with whom you have any level of contact. The second is a timeline of friendship that gives you a chance to remind yourself of past relationships and what they meant to you. The final sheet asks you to list your current relationships and think about each one's time and needs.

The aim of this Stocktake is to give consideration to all the people you spend time with, to evaluate how important those relationships are and to identify what sustenance they require to stay nurtured and happy. The Life Audit is not prescriptive. What it *does* do is get you to ask yourself a sequence of questions that will lead you to solutions to dilemmas you might have.

With an area of life as enormous as relationships, the

analysis will start at the very beginning of keeping your Time Log. They are a hugely important part of life, and concern about a relationship may well have been the trigger to embarking on this journey of self-discovery. Even if this wasn't your starting point, you'll find relationship issues will be interwoven with all other areas of your life and so will need addressing along the way.

For example, for me the triggers were my concerns about what defined me beyond my career and role as a mother and wife. For 29-year-old Charles it was how to make more, in pure financial terms he thought, of a wonderful but impecunious surfing lifestyle in Cornwall. For my thirty-something friend Suzanne it was whether to have a baby or pursue a career opportunity, and for 70-year-old retired George it was coming to terms with a day-to-day lifestyle that didn't involve large corporate responsibilities.

Regardless of the individual circumstances, for each of us life-changing decisions about relationships were part of the fallout from doing the Life Audit. For me it meant realigning the one with my husband and making a conscious decision to drop some friendships while making more of others. Charles had to face up to the fact that he lived a self-indulgent life as a beach bum which didn't offer much to any of the girls he dated, and that the real imperative behind his restlessness and desire to earn more was that he wanted to settle down and find that 'significant other'. Suzanne gave in to the ache for a baby and experienced both enormous relief at suspending the career move and a sudden softness and different, deeper love for her long-term partner. And George got rid of his hierarchical corporate hang-ups and got involved in community responsibilities, which made him some new friends amongst fellow governors of the local school and led in turn to new activities and new encounters that altered the pattern of his life.

The quality of your waking hours can often be measured by the company you keep, which is why your relationships need careful scrutiny from Day One of your Life Audit. Mention the word 'relationship' and we all think of family or friends. However, while the Life Audit does indeed help you to face up to the big questions surrounding those people, it also asks you to acknowledge your everyday encounters with others who are likely to play a lesser role in your life. This is why you will be making notes about everyone with whom you have any level of meaningful contact and describing the quality of those exchanges.

Of all the sections in the Life Audit, relationships may be the hardest to tackle – because, after all, what sort of person consciously decides to eliminate other people from their lives? Surely not the sort of person who deserves a loving family or friends in the first place? Trust me. It isn't as painful as you think. There is nothing more debilitating than a painful relationship that sucks your soul dry and leaves you feeling a lesser person. I've had those, and now I've been there and done it – done the Life Audit. I have put in perspective some family relationships and audited out certain other relationships. Once done it feels fantastic, and it is a wonderful confidence-builder! Most important of all, it rids you of time-consuming destructive associations. This in turn makes room for you to enjoy and enrich valued friendships and invest in new acquaintances to see if they have time to grow into important relationships.

We all have such high expectations of our partners,

children, parents, siblings and friends that it's not surprising that these are rarely met. Relationships can easily become fraught with emotion, making it even harder to sort out what's what. Many of us are very social these days and buddy up quickly with colleagues and acquaintances when in fact these relationships may not be more than passing encounters. Since life is usually already full in most other areas it makes practical sense to weigh up the social and emotional outlay you are prepared to invest (or maybe need) and then allocate the time accordingly. Believe me, once you move on to stage two and start matching available time with real-life demands in order to achieve the non-guilt-laden, happy balance that is your Breakeven position, you'll realise how much better it is to compartmentalise your relationships and identify which ones do require and deserve time and attention to prosper and which ones don't.

In a similar way to dealing with your health issues, the idea is for you to heed the subtle inner voices that acknowledge even the most low-key encounters of the kind which in the past you have not particularly noticed or placed any value upon. For instance, the duty receptionist at the gym may be the first person you exchange words with early each morning. Does that exchange enhance the moment or not? Does it have a value as a moment in your day? Is one person always so grumpy that it starts the day off on a real downer, or is there someone on a different shift who is always cheerful?

Making the notes and lists is invaluable, and what will emerge is an improving ability to 'read' what you really feel about people. You'll start to spot at ten paces the first dip of that sinking feeling when a friendship needs duty maintenance. Equally, you'll recognise instantly the small bubble of delight at the sight of someone's name in your email inbox or the sound of their voice on the end of the phone.

The better you read these signs, the easier you will find it to prioritise what really matters to you in relationship terms. And once you can accurately prioritise, then you can start making sure the important relationships really do get the necessary support and nurturing. Also – and this was the real bonus for me – you'll be able to spot and make room for new friendships that otherwise would have withered before they had a chance to blossom because there was no room, in other words quality time, available to devote to them.

The relationships you will be looking at can be divided into the following groups:

- *Partner*
- *Children*
- *Family*
- *Friends*
- *Colleagues*
- *Acquaintances*
- *Professionals (doctor, accountant etc.)*
- *Support services (cleaner, odd jobman etc.)*
- *Pets*

There will be plenty of anecdotal advice from people who have faced the same emotional dilemmas as you and down-to-earth advice where practical solutions are called for such as how to change your doctor or stop your cleaner intimidating you! In the past I've tied myself up in knots about those problems – but having applied the Life Audit to them, got them in perspective and finally solved them, I can strongly advocate a pragmatic and businesslike approach to getting rid of the particular grief they bring.

To complete the charts and Stocktake you will need to identify particular issues about your relationships, and during the days of collecting the data about your life you will be asked to note down the highs and lows of time spent with people. You will need to address a lot of issues to make sure you undertake an honest scrutiny of the strengths and weaknesses of your relationships with everyone in your life.

Ask yourself these questions:

- *Are you happy with this relationship?*
- *What life-enhancing qualities does this relationship bring?*
- *If this person suddenly vanished from your life, how would you feel?*
- *Where in your relationship league table does this person sit?*
- *Is this person part of a valued relationship only in certain areas of your life, i.e. do you share a particular interest?*
- *Do exchanges in the relationship ever make you feel sad?*
- *How balanced is the relationship?*
- *What do you think you mean to the other person?*
- *Is there a destructive aspect to the relationship?*
- *Do you feel duty-bound to maintain the relationship?*
- *If you knew then what you know now would you have cultivated the relationship when you first met?*
- *Do you wish you had set different ground rules for the way the relationship has developed?*
- *Is there an aspect of this relationship that could be improved?*
- *Are you content with the time and space you give this relationship?*

The first thing to do is to clarify *who* matters to you, and the Relationship Circle chart should first help you to put

First Stage

the people you care about in place around you. The principle is simple: you put yourself at the centre of your world of people and let them radiate out in groups determined by their closeness to you and degree of involvement in your life. You can compartmentalise them if you want to by placing family in one quarter, friends in another and so on. You may find you need to fill in the chart more than once, as time and circumstance shift the groups of people you spend time with, until you get a representative picture.

Simon, 23, found filling in this chart harder than he had thought. 'Because I'm not at college any more – I'm back at home thinking about what I'm going to do next – I found it hard to work out who all my friends are right now and where they fit into my life. At college I had dozens of mates and it would have been easy, but now it's hard to keep in contact with them all and in fact I'm seeing a lot of some of my old school friends who live locally. It's made me realise that I wasn't as close to some people as I thought I was, and that I'm likely to make a whole new circle of friends when life changes again. It's made me think about which people I really want to stay in touch with for the future, and why.'

The chart makes no assumptions about the order or closeness particular groups or individuals might have for you. It's up to you to decide who goes where. If friends are bigger in your life than family, they should go nearer you at the centre. Your dog or cat might be your most significant other at the moment. That's OK. Distant family might even come a close second to support services. After all, would you even recognise the cousin you only see at weddings and funerals if you passed him in the street? Write down what's true for you – it won't make you a bad person!

FILLING IN YOUR RELATIONSHIP CIRCLE

- *See chart 9.*
- *Make lists of the relationships you really care about in the lettered columns, categorising them if you want to, e.g. family in A, friends in B etc.*
- *The dot in the centre of the circle represents you. Next to it, write the name of the person who matters most to you.*
- *Add the names of family, friends, acquaintances and others to the rest of the circle, favouring those you care more for by placing them closer to the centre.*
- *Look at your daily encounters with colleagues and others, and see if the relationships you have with them are emotionally meaningful enough to feature in the circle.*
- *Don't ignore the obligatory relationships that you know you cannot relinquish because you accept that the commitment or connection is a fact of your life.*
- *Don't forget pets: they can fulfil a need to nurture and can be a great comfort at times of emotional crisis.*
- *Think of the circle representing radiating ripples of care and concern embracing those you have put in it.*

Now we come to something called your Relationship Timeline. Doing the Life Audit is such a time of self-reflection that it often prompts memories to come flooding back. This chart gives you the opportunity to trawl through your past and recall those friends and faces that were once important but may now have slipped out of your life. But be assured that this exercise isn't intended to make you feel you have let these people down. What it did for me, apart from making me get in touch with a few people I realised I actually wanted to see again, was something meaningful. It enabled me to appreciate how important some people had been at certain moments in time and how their friendship had enriched my life. It also reminded me how destructive one particular association had been, and how it had led me in a negative direction and caused unhappiness.

Overall I felt a dawning realisation of what different *sorts* of people meant to me, from my partner to those I worked with or interacted with on a more distant level. Filling in the timeline really did seem to put all my relationships, past and present, in perspective and help me to prioritise those people and relationships that were really important to me. It helped me define what I meant by 'friendship', which was useful when it came to making decisions further on in the Audit process.

Divorcee Joanne, still coming to terms with the break-up of her marriage and struggling to be optimistic about facing the future alone, found this process surprisingly constructive. 'I thought it would be depressing remembering all the friendships we'd made as a couple, on holiday and through the children. In fact, though, it proved to me how often I'd been the one to instigate relationships and that many had ceased to exist because of John's lack of enthusiasm. The ones that had survived were mainly where he had got on with the other man, and were not particularly ones that I would have fostered. It made me realise that I'm a sociable person in my own right and can now make friends with people *I* want to spend time with – including some that fell by the wayside in the past.'

FILLING IN YOUR RELATIONSHIP TIMELINE

- *See chart 10.*
- *Make as many copies as you need, which might be quite a few if you want to log lots of relationships.*
- *Make your entries in the boxes either side of the central vertical line, depending on whether they are positive or negative.*
- *Enter names, dates and give a brief description of the nature of the relationship, e.g. best friend.*
- *Think back to your earliest childhood memories of playmates.*
- *Chronologically work your way through the years at school. Remember where you played and what games.*
- *Recall your teenage years and who you had some of those first experiences with – staying out late, learning to drive, first dates and so on.*
- *Do the same thing with your adult years and walk yourself through the memories.*
- *Categorise the good and bad points of all the relationships.*
- *Don't shy away from acknowledging if a friendship or relationship was all bad or destructive.*
- *When you've reached the present day, spot any recurring characteristics of your relationships and include this in the defining statement.*

Now you've taken a close look at the people you currently interact with by drawing up your Relationship Circle, you need to produce a definitive Stocktake of those relationships which will include the time they demand and the nature of that time. You need to quiz yourself about how fulfilling or efficient the contact is, whether as a life-enhancing close relationship or as a functional aspect of day-to-day interaction. You also need to single out for attention any aspects of the relationship that need further consideration. For example, your relationship with your partner may on the whole be great but your sex life has gone off the boil. Or your relationship with your brother is fine on the surface but you never seem to talk about anything that really matters. This next Stocktake chart will determine the Breakeven position in terms of time that needs to be committed to relationships and is therefore not available for other things.

FILLING IN YOUR RELATIONSHIP STOCKTAKE: TIME AND NEEDS

- *See chart 11.*
- *Drawing the information from your Day Journals, Time Logs and the other two Relationship charts, list in column one the people you currently spend time with.*
- *In the second column, note which category of relationship it falls into, e.g. Family, Colleague, Support.*
- *Describe the typical use of time together one-on-one that sustains your relationship and note it in column three.*
- *Calculate the amount of dedicated time you spend with that person, outside day-to-day living or working alongside them. Take into account their expectations.*

- *Note any issues that may need addressing about a particular element of the relationship.*
- *Don't double account!*
- *Bear in mind that relationships that are professional or practical, such as support services, may and indeed should not need any one-on-one time outside the function they perform.*

Home Stocktake

Home as sanctuary, home as mortgage millstone, home as pit. What does your home mean to you? For myself I love 'home', wherever it is, and since my very first student digs I've been a nester. Bedsit, starter home or our present cottage, my home has always had to be a safe haven where I can batten down the hatches and be myself.

The aim of doing a Stocktake on your home is to define what it means to you, to catalogue the things you have in it and calculate how much of your life is currently taken up with looking after it and its contents. That amount of time will be the Breakeven that your current routine needs. The second stage of the Audit contains detailed and comprehensive advice on ways to improve the Breakeven figure – in other words to minimise that routine and release more time for you to devote to other matters. The two charts you will fill in are a property timeline and an inventory/checklist of your fixtures and fittings and your household chores and maintenance tasks.

Remember that the Audit resolutely doesn't attempt to tell you what you should own or what you should do.

That's why you have to make a current, *personal* situation report as the starting point for changes you may decide to introduce later to your life and routines. One person's castle is another person's pigsty, and who is to judge what is right and what is wrong for any individual? Everyone has different views on their homes and belongings. I have to have an emotional engagement with the actual bricks and mortar of my home; I think it's very important and comforting to be able to retreat from our big, challenging world of uncertainties and competitiveness into a familiar physical space. My husband, Mark, feels differently. He had a service family upbringing and, having had to move around so often as a child, feels that home is not so much a place but more a state of mind that can be created at any time and in any environment.

Jason, aged 25, had absolutely no comprehension why his home should be a Life Audit category. His shared house was simply where he slept when he was not 'living'. He was not needy in the 'homemaking' sense and didn't want it to be an expression of anything. It was as functional a part of his life as his toothbrush. Naomi, on the other hand, in her early thirties, poured enormous amounts of energy and love into her home surroundings. The mortgage on her maisonette was more than she could really afford, but that didn't inhibit her plans or her spending on imaginative decorating schemes. Her home seemed to be an outlet for a whole different side to Naomi, far removed from her job as a bank clerk. Then again Beryl, a 65-year-old widow, felt paralysed in the semi she and her husband had shared for 30 years. There seemed to her no point in replacing or renewing anything, and every room held a different sad memory. 'I've just got no energy or enthusiasm for the house,' she said. 'I feel completely uninterested in keeping it up, which is odd because I've always been quite houseproud.'

Each got something different out of doing the Audit. Jason made his home even more of a no-brainer by becoming more efficient and tidy, so that the place really was a holding and sleeping zone. Naomi identified and then sold some things she no longer needed, and put the proceeds into more interior decoration. Beryl felt reinvigorated and began to take a keener interest in her surroundings after confronting whether she should move from the family home; she decided not to, after the thought of leaving it made her appreciate it more.

Before you move on to filling in the Stocktake charts, consider for a moment whether you wrote anything about your home in your Really Personal Information. It might be worth keeping an eye on your thoughts about your surroundings to double-check how your feel about the house, flat or digs you live in, and amend or add to your wish list statement.

Your home may well be your biggest expense and the place you spend much of your time resting and recuperating. It's important to make sure it's where you want to be. Given all your other wishes, is there a better place or more suitable housing that might help you on your way or that would complement other dreams on your wish list? It may be that your mortgage outlay is keeping you trapped in a job you hate and in a property that is in turn sapping your energy and disposable income for other activities. Or it may be that either urban or rural life has lost its appeal and that you will need to change your lifestyle and location fundamentally in order to reflect your changing ambitions. Try to examine your thoughts, in terms of both wishes and regrets in your Really Personal

Information entries, on how you feel about the physical place you inhabit.

Ask yourself these questions:

- *What do you like about your home?*
- *What depresses you about your home?*
- *Does the cost of your home fit your budget?*
- *Does it feel like a sanctuary?*
- *What makes it feel like a sanctuary?*
- *Does it reflect your style?*
- *Has it a distinct atmosphere, smell, feel about it?*
- *What words (e.g. beautiful, practical, sunny, cosy) describe it?*
- *Does living in this home affect you – is it making its mark on you?*
- *Is your home a part of your life that reinforces or helps define you?*
- *If you had to move tomorrow, how would you feel about leaving this home?*

It helps to look back over the places you have lived in throughout your life, and the Home Timeline will allow you to focus on what it is in your domestic set-up that makes you happy or miserable. Home can be either sanctuary or hellhole, and for most of us it is the single most important environment in terms of either enhancing our life or bringing us down. Looking back on where you have lived, do you remember how depressing that student flat was in your second year at university and how you loathed returning to it so much that you moved out after a term? Do you remember the excitement of getting the keys to the first place you actually owned? You need to be able to identify the pluses and minuses of your surroundings and apply the same criteria to places where you have lived in the past. By looking back over former homes, almost as an outsider watching someone else changing and evolving at their various life stages, you will start to get more of a sense of who you are, of your needs and of your relationship with your home.

FILLING IN YOUR HOME TIMELINE

- *See chart 12.*
- *You're going to log every place you've lived in for any significant time.*
- *Use the prompt boxes to write each one down in the boxes either side of the central vertical line.*
- *Enter the location and 'from' and 'to' dates.*
- *Add words that describe good and bad aspects of the property and your time in it if you want.*
- *Come up with a statement about what your home means to you.*

Now, what about the stuff you have in this very important place, your home? 'Stuff' isn't a very fetching word for the precious belongings you have accumulated and draw comfort from. But if you are anything like me and most other people who have done the Life Audit you are likely to have loads of things in your home that qualify as 'stuff'. There'll be stuff in drawers, under beds, in cupboards, under the stairs, in the shed and cluttering up the garage. Stuff you have bought or been given that might or might not have once had a purpose and that hasn't been touched for months or even years. Stuff that needs

First Stage

cleaning, putting back in place, maintaining. But you are now going to make a definitive list of your home's fixtures and fittings from bricks and mortar, windows and carpets to appliances and ornaments.

This process will quite literally put your house in order. Take that great quote from the nineteenth-century design guru and social reformer William Morris: 'Have nothing in your house that you do not know to be useful or believe to be beautiful.' That is as good a criterion as any to assess your belongings against if you are dithering over whether something has a place in your life. Don't forget, beauty is in the eye of the beholder. *You* are that beholder. Who cares if antimacassars are out! If you love them, cherish them, write them down.

Surprisingly, this process doesn't take as long as you might think. What it does immediately highlight is how much superfluous 'stuff' you may have. Take the bedroom: once I'd written down 'bed, linen, curtains, wardrobe, dressing table, bedside tables and lamps' – which, let's face it, is pretty much all you need in a bedroom – there wasn't much to add, apart from a picture I love and a mirror, plus some wicker baskets that hold my make-up and a potted plant. Basically, your list should consist of things you can see if you stand in the doorway to each room; don't worry at the moment about what's inside cupboards and closets.

Ask yourself these questions:

- *What do you do in this room?*
- *Which items do you use in this room that are directly related to that activity?*
- *Which items are incidental?*
- *Do you really* love *any surplus items?*

- *Do any surplus items have other uses unconnected with this room, and if so should they live somewhere else?*

As with your diet and fitness, you may want to start the adjustments immediately and be keen to start de-cluttering as you consider each room. That's fine, and if you are compelled to, remove anything that you are confident is neither beautiful nor useful to you. Be aware, though, that the business of sorting out your life is still work in progress, so you may want to postpone any *drastic* chucking until the next stage of the Audit.

Try to find a holding area for rejected stuff, such as a spare room or garage, that will see you through the Audit time. This will allow you to reinstate any items that you decide you want to keep after all, if you have been over-zealous in your de-cluttering. If not, either bite the bullet, junk the item and live with the possible consequences of realising you really did love or need it, or push it into a corner, literally and mentally, to be dealt with when you have completed the Stocktake.

You should end up with a definitive list of the main goods and chattels in each room of your home. But now what? Think about the cleaning and maintenance of these selected accessories of your life. They may be useful or beautiful, but if they are grubby or broken they might also become a negative. Before doing the Audit I constantly berated myself about the dust and muck my 'stuff' accumulated, which made my home a more complicated aspect of my life than the comfort zone I longed for it to be. While it is indeed my patch, where I can let my hair down and be truly relaxed in the course of a busy life, my home was also for a time one of life's battlegrounds: I was fighting a war to exercise the control and order over the

First Stage

housework that I was spectacularly failing to do in the rest of my life.

Anyone who has a problem with the idea that a book that's claiming it may change your life is addressing housework should think again. Call me sad, call me ridiculous, just don't tell me I'm alone when I say, hand on heart, that some of my happiest moments have been when all my household appliances were going at once on a Saturday morning. One load in the washing machine, another already in the tumble drier, the dishwasher rinsing the breakfast dishes (and probably last night's supper plates), the breadmaker kneading bread for lunch and the happy sound of a child or husband hoovering somewhere. Joy. The whirr, hum and grind of order! *That* cup of coffee was the best of the week. *Then* I could relax.

But when the family all left, I realised that my control freakery in the housework department was rather pointless when there was no one to tidy up after. I think as well that my friends, and my family in particular, looked on in bemusement as I succeeded in making my home spectacularly muddled and chaotic at the same time as being neurotic about the mess. I'm sure a psychologist would have something to say about it but it seems pretty obvious to me, looking back, that the housework was one area I *could* sort and so I made sure there was always enough of a muddle to keep me busy.

Apparently, housework is the new black, the new sex, the new going out and most definitely something that stars like Madonna and Kylie are happy to talk about doing. But putting fashion aside, in the same way that shedding outdated belongings can liberate you from the past, so looking after your current belongings can give you security in the present and a kind of clarity.

Housework *is* important, whoever you are, whatever age or sex you are. I defy anyone not to agree that having a tidy home is a positive rather than a negative. It doesn't need to be neat and boring with everything uniformly in place. It doesn't actually need to be any more tidy and clean than *you* need it to be to get a calm, contented, sorted feeling that allows you to make the most of 'being' in your safe haven, sleeping space, creative outlet, call it what you will. It's your home, it's where you lay your head – it should not cause you any grief.

A few years ago there was a popular print doing the rounds that carried the caption: 'A tidy house equals a dull woman.' To be honest, I found this rather a comfort, and certainly an excuse as, given my losing battle with the housework, it was easy to decide that I'd rather be interesting than tidy any day. But then I was put in my place by a French friend of mine who found this statement insulting. Françoise's home is stylish, individual and eclectically tidy. She doesn't ever appear to make a meal out of housework, yet at one stage had three teenagers living under her roof and entertained weekly while holding down a full-time job. She illustrated the point that, even with high standards and other commitments and no matter how busy you are, order and organisation can give you the optimum housework routine.

I think it would be impossible for me to put the amount of energy into my home as Françoise does, and I'm pretty sure I wouldn't be able to sustain it. But what I did want to do with the Life Audit was to find a realistic, manageable position where the tidying and cleaning was straightforward. I want to be more than little Miss Houseproud and therefore I wanted to compartmentalise my housework so that it was done to a standard I was happy with – but I

First Stage

89

didn't spend all my time doing it.

If your home is high on your list of priorities you may choose to spend more time on this area than others in your Stocktake. Everyone has elements of the house or housework that they are fanatical about, and everyone has what they consider to be their benchmark level of tidiness and cleanliness. The Stocktake is the chance to write down what input you need to make in order to reach your personal level.

Ask yourself these questions:

- *What housework do you consider imperative?*
- *Do you have a system or routine for doing the housework?*
- *Do you do the housework at a regular time?*
- *Are you selective about the products you use?*
- *Have you prioritised rooms?*
- *Have you prioritised chores?*
- *Do you aim to hit your gold standard all the time?*
- *Do you expect others to help?*
- *Do they help?*

As you stocktake each room, look beyond the cleaning – think about maintenance, too, and note down any regular or outstanding jobs such as painting a window frame or replacing a broken tile. At this stage you shouldn't be cataloguing creative redecoration plans. If you have a burning desire to make-over your bedroom it should be on the wish list in your Really Personal Information, and will be taken into consideration later in the Audit process.

Don't forget the amount of time you spend on non-cleaning chores such as laundry, domestic administration, cooking, clearing up after the family and so on. Certain aspects of gardening (mowing the lawn, cutting the hedges) may come into this category, as opposed to those that you might conceivably regard as leisure activities, such as planting. Treat car maintenance similarly. Collect the average weekly commitment from your daily Time Logs and Day Journals, and calculate them across your chosen Audit period.

FILLING IN YOUR HOME STOCKTAKE

- *See chart 13.*
- *Tackle this task room by room.*
- *Really scrutinise each room's contents and, apart from cupboard or drawer contents, don't miss out anything, however obvious.*
- *Use the opportunity to note down things you can get rid of or essential things you need to buy.*
- *Don't lay claim to a textbook super-clean standard if you know you don't and won't achieve it.*
- *Note down the daily, weekly, etc. tasks that get the house to a state you are satisfied with.*
- *Refer to the Day Journals for other domestic duties such as laundry and domestic administration, and note down the time they take.*
- *Consider the property's essential maintenance needs and account for them too.*
- *Total up the time you have calculated you need to look after your house and its contents – don't double account.*
- *Use the statement box to sum up how you feel about this aspect of your life.*

Image Stocktake

What is 'image?' Is it a tangible, *real* thing or is it something you create – a gloss, a superficial pretence? Who needs an image? With such honest brokering going on while you are auditing your life, surely you should be peeling away any subterfuge that masks the reality of you?

Really, your image is not as personal a thing as you might think. Of course, your self-image – your perception of yourself – is something that matters enormously, especially during this navel-gazing time, but this section of the book is just as much about the outward-facing persona you present to the world. You only have to think of the messages that uniforms – military, medical or religious – send out, or of how a simple wedding ring indicates your married state, to know not to underestimate the power of appearance.

The world of business and finance understands very well the importance of other people's perceptions in fostering effective working relationships and in closing deals. One company I know of insists that its consultants travel to appointments only by train and taxi; if they take their own car they have to leave it around the corner. The same company also bans old school ties. The idea is to avoid the risk of clients being either aggrieved or alienated by the external accoutrements of the person they're dealing with. Have you ever thought about the messages your appearance sends out?

Ask yourself these questions:

- *Is your overall look typical of someone of your age or profession?*
- *What clues does your appearance give about the sort of*

person you are?

- *Are you conscious that your appearance is a mismatch with the real you?*
- *Do you feel pressurised to look a certain way and to conform?*
- *Do you prefer an anonymous look?*
- *If so, do you think that is because you lack confidence in your sense of style?*
- *Do you know what image you would like to have?*

An anthropologist friend once told me that when each and every one of us looks in the mirror, however poor our body image is, our eyes will still be drawn to our best feature and we will see ourselves, at least in that aspect, as beautiful. There is a reverse to this too, of course, when you are over-conscious of a blemish that feels the size of a mountain but that no one else notices. Both extremes involve a degree of denial, but while doing the Audit it would be good to peer honestly into your looking glass and quite literally see yourself in all your glory but *with* the warts and all.

Your image is essentially the way you style yourself. Your styling is a combination of the clothes you wear and the way you look after your body and hair – in other words your wardrobe and your grooming routines. You are going to stocktake these two elements that make up your style and work out what you've got, what you do and what you need, getting as far back to basics as that proverbial sock drawer we've been talking about since the start of the Audit.

There are three charts, one for your clothes, one for your grooming routine and one to help you define your style and look.

Clothes

Have you ever walked along a street and, catching sight of someone's reflection in a shop window, taken a second or two to realise it's you? What, me? That plump person, stooped person, person in the dowdy clothes! God, how did *that* happen? It was never meant to be like this – *I* was never meant to look like this. It's that self-denial thing again. The actuality of the way we look, dress and present ourselves in public can be a long way removed from the image we have in our mind. Our 'look' may have evolved over years with changing circumstances, and we have just not noticed that the reality is nothing like the picture we carry around in our heads. I think we all have a moment in time that defines the look we keep in our mind's eye. For me, it's the end of my teens when I was a bit of a hippie and loved the clothes.

My own 'How did that happen?' moment came at the beginning of doing the Audit as I put on a particular business suit. It's a smart, sharply cut little number with a short, fitted skirt and jacket. I was headed for a long train journey and then a meeting, and it was ideal because it was made out of some miracle modern fabric that wouldn't crease. But I suddenly realised I hated it! It looked fine and it certainly served its 'work uniform' purpose because it doesn't crease and is typical formal wear. But where had that happy hippie gone? There wasn't a trace of her looking back at me from the mirror. I know she's plumper and older and a lot less dreamy now, but surely she was never destined for short, sharp skirts in man-made fabrics, was she?

It got me thinking. Money, my employers, my position and fashion all had bearings on my choice of clothes, but along the way I'd lost sight of the look I *wanted* to portray.

Or maybe not lost sight of it – just not thought about it or really given it any time. Surely that young girl, grown older, would have wanted to adapt the style that she loved and that reflected her personality? But she'd just got too busy and tired and distracted to find a creative compromise.

Peter, just retired, felt downright confused about his clothes choices. Working in an office for the last 45 years, he had grown accustomed to a daily uniform of suits and ties. His new freedom gave him the opportunity to loosen up his look, but instead he found himself simply replicating his weekend casuals. He wasn't quite sure how he wanted his image to change, and carrying out the Audit helped define this. 'It made me realise how conservative I was about wearing *appropriate* clothes, and that retiring was in fact a chance to stop playing by other people's rules. When I worked, even my casual clothes were an extension of the conformity I exhibited elsewhere. I hope this doesn't sound too ridiculous, but I've found I enjoy wearing colours. In particular, some red cords! They've caused some raised eyebrows at the pub.'

Martin, now 49, was also rather rueful when talking about his days of long hair, loon pants and velvet jackets in the mid 1970s. He loved that look, and felt that he was a much funkier, freer person then than he is now. As an account manager for a large department store he has to conform at work, but he realised sadly that his out-of-work clothes were as unfunky as he himself had become. 'I have become *so* dull. It was interesting to examine my look and plan a fresh start with a cooler out-of-work set of clothes.'

Of course people change, grow up, put aside the whimsies of youth and conform. Also, life delivers up the practical necessities of 'being appropriate' and that applies enormously to outward appearance, especially at work.

But your image is the visible manifestation of *you*. It's important to ally some honesty to all that practicality in order to reinforce and restate the person you are.

Since clothes probably make the biggest statement about your image, it's easy to start the Image Stocktake with them. Over the course of the Life Audit you will be writing down on your daily summary the clothes you wear each day. When you come to do your Stocktake it will then be an easy exercise to work out which outfits went with what events, occasions and circumstances, and to come up with a definitive list of the contents of your active wardrobe which will enable you to eliminate the clothes that never get worn.

This is where your sock drawer comes into the Audit because socks, their drawer and its tidiness becoming a given rather epitomises the Audit ethos. A tidy, sorted sock drawer means you don't waste a second more than is essential on choosing and putting on socks. Socks and the order of their keeping are all part of 'image'.

Ask yourself these questions:

- *Given the day's agenda, what outfits can you choose from?*
- *Why did one outfit get preference over other suitable ones?*
- *Would you always choose that outfit given the same events?*
- *If you have more than one outfit suitable for an occasion, will you genuinely ring the changes?*
- *Why do you bypass some outfits despite their suitability?*
- *Are some of your surplus clothes simply not being selected during the Audit because the season is wrong?*
- *Are there clothes that are either too big or too small in your wardrobe?*

- *Be honest about whether you will definitely wear the glad rags at the back of the wardrobe for a special occasion.*

There will probably be a load of clothes that you haven't worn for a while and which you need to look over with a critical eye and match them against your life. If you can't bear the thought of chucking them immediately, store them somewhere until you are fully and finally convinced how very much simpler life is without them cluttering up your clothes choices each morning.

While it's fine to adjust the way you dress throughout the month of your Audit, try not to make any radical changes such as going out and buying a whole new wardrobe because now is definitely not the time to decide on definitive shifts. That will come after the Stocktake when you will be much clearer about who you are and what messages you want your outward appearance to send out or reinforce. Like every other aspect of your life your wardrobe, including the sock drawer, is a work in progress.

You will also need to record the amount of time you spent planning and shopping for your clothes, taken from the Daily Time Logs. But, as was the case with me and cooking, you need to make sure that time spent on your wardrobe doesn't fall into the category of leisure. Remember that this is not necessarily how you want your wardrobe to look in the final reckoning, but rather a Stocktake of what you have and wear *now*, and in listing it there is no room for self-delusion.

Grooming

Now it's time to examine the other elements which make up your look. In your Daily Time Log you will be noting down how long you spend each day on 'personal' stuff such as your grooming routine. Quite apart from the pleasure you may derive from this in image terms, your personal grooming is as important as any other aspect of presenting yourself to the world. And this applies even if you are a quick 'sh*t, shower and shave' merchant, as one ex-boyfriend of mine used to describe himself. As with all other areas, you need to look at yourself and decide what needs to be done, when, and what tools of the trade you need to do it, as well as how long it takes and how often it should happen.

You'll already be clocking the time you spend and how you spend it, but I also think that at some point it's worth taking time out to contemplate your navel in the bathtub – literally. Run yourself a good deep bath, even if you prefer to shower. Take the opportunity of some soaking time to consider fully what you do to enhance your body beautiful in the personal hygiene and aesthetic sense. While the water is running, gather together all the bathing or grooming products you regularly use. Then, lying in the bath, scrutinise your body just as you did in the health process. Contemplate your hair, your skin, your face, your teeth and your hands, feet and nails. Now note what you do, with what and how long it takes. Afterwards continue with whatever routine you would normally follow and write down the lotions, creams, appliances or make-up you use.

Ask yourself these questions:

- *How much conscious thought do you give to the things you do and the products you use?*
- *Can you remember why you chose such and such a product or make of appliance?*
- *Are you doing a certain part of your routine because you consider it essential, or because you get a separate sensory pleasure?*
- *If so, would you be prepared to sacrifice the enjoyment element to reduce the things you do and the time it takes you?*
- *Do you have different products or routines for different types of day or event?*

First Stage

The completed Stocktake form is a sort of grooming template which can be added to. Start refining it by, for example, keeping separately just the stuff you use and seeing if you ever seek out the other make-up colours, appliances or products you possess. When you do your Stocktake you should end up with a tally of things that are in use; the rest can be chucked, stored or given to friends.

Style

Now for something a little less precise that you need to achieve in your Stocktake of image. What you need to do is accurately to define and refine what your look is and how happy you are with it. Did this feature at all on your wish list? Possibly not. But wanting to look your best, and to let the statement that your appearance makes about the person you are be an honest and reinforcing one, is as much part of the person you are as your social conscience or career ambition – and it's a really easy fix. As you become more aware of the processes and routines you follow with your clothes, grooming and products, start quizzing yourself about how removed they are from the look and image you want to portray.

Ask yourself these questions:

- *Can you define the look you would love to have?*
- *How near is your current appearance to the mind's eye picture you have of yourself that you want or hope to display to the outside world?*
- *Is there a famous person whose look you would like to emulate?*
- *Are there colours you particularly like?*
- *What are the winning elements of different outfits that you know work well for you?*

Doing this will make you automatically more aware of other people's success with style. Look at others on the bus, in the pub or at work. Consider the different types of people portrayed on television or in magazines, and start rejecting or contemplating 'looks' depending on how close they are to the sort of image you want to give.

Money Stocktake

Money should by rights be the easiest part of your life to audit, because after all it 'owns' the jargon we're using. However, it is also one of the most important and contentious areas of life. It's not just what you do with it that matters, but how you manage it, your access to credit, the servicing of any debt and the growth of your savings and investments. To stocktake your money you need to work out to what extent your income matches your expenditure, and to come up with a figure that represents your total worth. This section contains suggestions on how to improve the Breakeven figure by maximising the use of your money while cutting down the time it takes you to manage, and there are lots of tips on how to think laterally about your earning potential, how to save money and how to speed up your personal accounting.

Money can be a powerful force that sets you free; equally, it can keep you trapped in an unhappy situation. It's emotive and complicated, and it's a bald fact of life that it is a difficult thing to marshal, both in terms of the getting and spending of it, and of your attitude towards it.

Sheila and Brian thought that stocktaking their finances would be a straightforward aspect of the Audit because they were both on fixed incomes, had no debts and managed their affairs tidily. 'Not so!' said Sheila. 'Things got quite heated, because once we started talking about what we wanted in the future it was clear that either one of us would have to earn more, or we'd have to think about cutting our costs or borrowing against the house. The conversation became more about our money than about our lives, and we had to really work at it to sort out our priorities.'

Wayne, 30, said he started to think in terms of what *time* he had to 'spend' earning in order to buy drinks in the pub on a Friday night. 'It was a sobering thought that my weekly session with my mates cost four life hours to earn the money it cost, on top of the time we spent supping. It threw a whole new light on how good the beer and the chat had to be.'

Unless you have a specific interest in financial management, money in terms of the Audit is simply a facilitator of other aspects of life. It helps keep you clothed and fed, and if you are lucky might fund a couple of steps on your way to achieving an ambition. Working through the Audit process will also reveal whether the earning of it or the keeping of what you've got is any sort of ball and chain.

Ask yourself these questions:

- *How much of a worry is your financial state of affairs?*
- *Does it colour every decision or plan you currently make?*
- *Do you have rows with a partner about it?*
- *Do you know exactly what your financial position is?*
- *How often do you balance your books?*

You will undoubtedly have your own accounting system already, even if it's just a shoe box in the corner of your bedroom where you chuck old receipts and cheque book stubs. Ask yourself what your money management system is. Does it, in its current form, cause sporadic chaos? If so, what does that fall-out time cost you across a typical year? Any VAT-registered businessperson knows only too well what a nightmare it can be when a return needs to be filed if you haven't kept a close track of your buying and selling and kept all the receipts. Even for the ordinary person, ordering goods on a credit account by mail order and not hanging on to the return slips can treble the amount of time spent dealing with the person in the call centre querying your order.

If you haven't done a personal budget before, you may need to do a bit of foraging in your files to get some accurate figures. The first chart in this section is designed to assess frankly and honestly how much you earn and what you spend your income on. You won't be analysing the rights or wrongs of either of these things at this stage – remember, this is just a process aimed at achieving a current situation report which will *then* lead on to making informed changes. (Mind you, if you currently buy four lattes a day from Starbuck's and one of your moans is a shortage of disposable income, I bet you find you cut down your coffee consumption.)

FILLING IN YOUR MONEY STOCK-TAKE: INCOME AND EXPENDITURE

- *See chart 17.*
- *It should account for money over a year.*
- *The headings on the left are the sources of income and the subjects of expenditure.*
- *Enter in the middle column the items of expenditure incurred in each category.*
- *Now, in the right hand column, enter against each of these the amounts spent.*
- *Make sure they are as accurate as possible by going over payslips, expenditure receipts and bank statements for the last 12 months.*
- *Total the income entries.*
- *Total up the expenses.*
- *Subtract expenses from income to see what (if anything) you have left over.*

So that's the coming and going of money. Now for an interesting chart which will determine your net worth. You may not feel this applies to you, but it's a reality check to establish what assets you would have if you cleared any debts and sold all your fixtures and fittings. In other words, what money would you have in your hand if you stood there in your stockinged feet and that pair of socks was all you owned. That money is 'chips-down' money. That money is 'drive into the sunset' money. That money may well be 'running away' money, or it may be the figure you need to know in order to make some big, life-changing decisions.

First Stage

Work Stocktake

This is a challenging part of your life to audit, because you may feel you don't have much control over the time you are spending at your job. The company that employs you dictates what you do and when, and your performance and success are measured by how well you meet the company's expectations. But 'work', of course, doesn't just mean a 'job'. Work can be more broadly defined as something you have to do each day, and therefore means different things to different people. If you are a student it will mean study. If you are a stay-at-home mum it's the hours you put in looking after your kids. If you are unemployed it's the time you commit to job-seeking. And if you are retired it's the routine things you have taken responsibility for, which may well cross over into other areas such as money management or home or support services.

Not only is work something that probably takes up a large proportion of your time, it is most likely also something that funds the rest of your life and supports you and your family. Decisions about it will have far-reaching consequences, so you must think hard about your level of commitment to it and the importance it has in your life and those of others. However, there are parts of your working day that you can reclaim, and you may also find that the pattern of your working life is not as inflexible as it first appears. You can and should consider how fulfilled and satisfied you are with your career choice, what prospects it offers and whether, given other life decisions you may be making, it is the right position or even career for you. Be realistic, too, about your standing in your business, whatever it is. Are your skills up-to-date? Are your employers likely to be looking for a younger, fitter, cheaper or more up-to-date model? And could redundancy be looming?

There are two charts to help you stocktake your work. The first looks at how your hours are taken up and the degree of flexibility they offer, and charts the fulfilment and satisfaction ratio. Since most people's jobs take up a huge chunk of their life, it's crucial that those hours really are accounted for at every level: practical, personal and emotional. The second chart challenges you to assess your performance and prospects. Those who have career interests centre stage and are competitive and ambitious will be keen to make the most of every working minute as part of their strategy for advancement. If this applies to you, it is essential you are aware of it when considering the place that work occupies in your life.

Dissatisfaction with your work can be as powerful a trigger for a major life change as an unhappy relationship.

Confusion about career choices can cause muddle in other life areas such as money, home life and relationships. Several twenty-somethings echoed Tim's position. 'I managed to get a job soon after leaving college, but after a couple of years wasn't sure it was what I wanted to do for the rest of my life. My degree had been in geography and the job was with a bank. The money was OK and there were promotion prospects but I just didn't feel it was *me* – where I really wanted to be.' Tim carried out the Audit and was able to identify the cause of his restlessness as regret that he hadn't fitted in more travel between school, university and employment. He plans to try to keep the door open to be able to return to the bank, maybe in another capacity, after he's cured his wanderlust.

Carrie, 37, had thrown herself into her career and up until a couple of years previously had enjoyed her work as a television producer. 'Suddenly it wasn't what I wanted to do. I couldn't stop hankering for a change and couldn't put my finger on why. Doing the Audit made me realise it was because I'd reached a sort of career ceiling. My work would be more of the same for the foreseeable future, and I wanted to do something radically different. I'm now training to be a yoga instructor and hope to start up a small business in that while keeping some TV work going on a freelance basis.'

Ask yourself these questions:

- *Do you look forward to going to work?*
- *If so, can you pinpoint why?*
- *Are you paid a fair amount for the job you do?*
- *Is your salary the main motivation for doing this particular job?*
- *Which aspect of your work do you most like?*

- *What do you dislike about your work?*
- *Are you happy with the hours you work?*
- *Can you predict what you will be doing in your job in six months, a year, five years?*
- *Are you aware of any scope for flexible hours, taking a sabbatical, job-sharing?*

What you may also find yourself doing is introducing greater order and clarity into the personal work patterns that you *can* control. This will be useful if, despite recognising a level of dissatisfaction in your working life, you are not able to consider a change in employment for financial or family reasons. One of the options I considered, but eventually rejected, was to come to terms with my own job dissatisfaction and to compartmentalise my day, really making the most of life outside work. And that non-work time was to include lunchtime and coffee breaks. I would have been able to reclaim a lot of time for myself and my other interests, and part of the plan would have been to add value to the hours 'around' work and just take the money for the job. This would have reduced the job to the status of an enabler for the rest of my ambitions. However, that wasn't the right option for me because I had a very specific need to be challenged by my actual work.

I felt that my work wasn't giving me back the reward I expected and that I was sacrificing 'life' in the process. Many other people who have done the Life Audit say the same kind of thing: reaching their career goals had not made them happy. It's not that they wanted to retire or downshift but rather that they were seeking something more – a personal reward rather than just a fat salary or high position. Inevitably, though, it's a big deal to give up on a successful career and to walk away from a level of income you have arrived at through hard work and experience and have, frankly, got used to!

Gill, in her early fifties and recovering from breast cancer, said she felt desperately torn between a job she enjoyed running a charity and the need to break free and do something different. 'It's taken me years to build up this level of security, and it feels foolhardy to chuck it all in, but. . . .' She eventually managed to get nine months' sabbatical leave and moved to the country to spend that time writing. The desire to escape can strike at any age, although the crucial times, I think, are in the mid to late twenties and thirties and in the mid-forties, as happened to me. I experienced a sense of 'working' time running out and a need to find new opportunities, driven by different motives. But simply leaving one job doesn't necessarily mean you will walk into something better, and so if there's a problem you really have to understand what is making you dissatisfied with your current work set-up.

FILLING IN YOUR WORK STOCKTAKE: TIME COMMITMENT/ JOB SATISFACTION

- *See chart 19.*
- *Mark off the hours you give over to work each day.*
- *Identify travelling time.*
- *Write down along the bottom line against the hours the particular activity you are engaged on.*
- *On the vertical line, assess on a scale of 1–10 your level of job satisfaction.*

- Consider whether you enjoy your work because of the job itself.
- Are there external influences causing you to question your level of job satisfaction?
- Are you happy with your work/life balance?
- Do you like your colleagues?
- Do this exercise enough times to supply a reasonable average.
- The purpose of this chart is twofold: to pragmatically assess your time commitment to work, but also to understand how that commitment makes you feel.
- Don't forget to finish with a statement about how your work defines you (or not).

Of course, it may be the long-term prospects of your job or career that concern you; not least because, often, your professional destiny may seem to be vulnerable to the vagaries of the business world, industrial trends, or out-of-sight bosses and accountants. All the more need, then, to be very honest with yourself about what your work portfolio looks like and have a shot at anticipating the good and bad factors that may determine your working future. The Performance and Prospects chart offers a chance to write an accurate situation report on your current standing and to give some consideration to what the future holds.

Leisure Stocktake

How does one define leisure? I think leisure is whatever allows you to chill. It doesn't necessarily have to have a purpose – it's the areas of your life that allow you to relax but don't have to tie in with specific, conscious 'relax' time as in meditation or having an afternoon nap. As far as leisure is concerned, one person's gym routine is another person's workout with the TV remote. Stocktaking your leisure time seeks to identify how much time you give to leisure and what form it takes.

Several people I spoke to initially misunderstood the Audit as an exercise in identifying purely 'me' time. But as you'll have gathered by now, that is not the case – your ultimate use of the free time you manage to identify is just as likely to involve other people as not. But of all the categories of life you are examining and stocktaking, leisure is probably the nearest you'll get to a self-focused use of time, although many people find their greatest relaxation when they are with others and in particular caring for them.

Sharon, a 43-year-old mother of two, said she would never feel completely relaxed without her family, and didn't enjoy holidays or free time at weekends without her husband and sons. 'Maybe it's because I work full-time, but a perfect leisurely day for me would be pottering around at home with everyone around, cooking a slap-up meal and watching a DVD together in the evening.' Amber, in her mid-thirties, worried about whether she made her leisure time too busy. 'I seem to fill my free time with lots of things and people which I enjoy, but then I sort of keel over every couple of weeks because there's no slack in my leisure time – no easy time. I spend a lot of time feeling guilty about not training at the gym or not seeing friends. All the things I class as leisure are things I feel I must do. I think I need to reassess what I really mean by leisure.'

Charlie, in his mid-forties, was surprised when he looked at his time use and realised that he could class the time he spent looking after his classic Morgan car as leisure. 'That's been a revelation. There are very few things I do that are just for the sheer joy of it, and it was an easy cliché to see cleaning the car as a weekly chore. But in fact I get real satisfaction from doing it, and it's possibly the

First Stage

113

most relaxing hour of my week.' Like Charlie, I discovered that leisure can be found in unusual places. For instance, I spend a lot of time cooking and for the first few days of my own Life Audit was dutifully entering the number of hours I spent in the kitchen under the heading 'domestic'. But then it dawned on me that actually I didn't want to cut down on that time, and eventually I had to move it from a 'domestic' chore to a 'relax' entry when I clocked how much pleasure I got from it. Similarly, 'relax' time for some people may be gardening, but much as I like wandering around the flower beds dead-heading the roses, heavy-duty digging leaves me cold. It's important to be quite specific about which category activities like these fall into for *you*.

When you look at the long-term picture for your Balance Sheet that will identify the free time you can draw down to plan how you are going to achieve a big ambition, don't forget bank holidays and the like. If they are times when you remove yourself from the daily duties of life, then they are most definitely times for leisure. Leisure may also be just what lets you off the hook of responsibility. So sometimes it's spending time with friends, at other times it's real solitude. It's the treat stuff of life, the moments that make you glow with contentment.

Ask yourself these questions:

- *When did you last feel totally relaxed?*
- *Where were you?*
- *What elements made up that moment?*
- *How often do you have leisure time?*
- *How often do you have holidays?*
- *What, if anything, do you have to be* doing *to feel relaxed?*

- *Do you mainly spend your leisure time alone or in company?*
- *Does your leisure time cross over into other life areas?*
- *Do you have to make time for leisure?*
- *Is leisure a priority or is it the first thing to get cancelled?*

The Stocktake asks you to define where you find your leisure and to identify what it is in your life that allows you to unwind and relax.

FILLING IN YOUR LEISURE STOCKTAKE

- *See chart 21.*
- *Write down in the first column what activity or non-activity makes you relaxed.*
- *Calculate how much time you are able to give this form of leisure.*
- *Identify whether there is any crossover into another life area such as going for a walk (fitness?) while chatting to friends.*
- *Consider whether the leisure activity or event brought added value. For example, did you learn something really fascinating through reading or watching television, or did a relationship get particularly nurtured or boosted through time spent with a friend?*
- *Finally, write a defining statement about the leisure you get in your life and your attitude to it.*

Citizenship Stocktake

The Audit is all about prioritising, and you are doing that by putting yourself at the centre of your personal world and looking closely at your relationship with everything that touches your own life. But what about the bigger picture? Do you play any part in making the wider world a better place? You are trying to get the minutiae of your life right so that you can concentrate on bigger things that matter. Well, they don't get much bigger than this!

What is citizenship? For me, it was a guilty conscience. As I looked closely at my own life I realised how inward-looking I was – I did hardly anything outside my own little existence to make the world a better place. Sure I thought about it occasionally, usually in the car when something came on the radio that pricked my somnolent social conscience about starving children or the neglected elderly or the environment. But I'd probably be on my way to do a big shop at the supermarket and, while aware that I should do something, somehow I would manage to put it on the mental pending pile to deal with another day.

Helen's parents had been actively involved in social issues, but she felt that her own efforts were but a pale imitation. 'They were very much people of their generation in the fifties and sixties, and the talk in our house was all about helping others. The focus for me is much more about my own family and our own needs, although I do care about what goes on in the world. I suppose I feel guilty because I hold myself up against my parents. Or perhaps my attitude is a reaction to them.'

While the overall Audit exercise is all about taking responsibility for our own lives and happiness, most of us would also like to include an element of collective charge for making the world a better place. But it's so easy *not* to be a player on any stage greater than that of our own little world. Global communications technology now brings wars and famines and peace processes right into our living rooms on a daily basis, but does that also in a way desensitise us? So at this stage in the Audit, while you may feel you have absolutely nothing in your current make-up to stocktake in terms of citizenship, it might be useful to assess how great a sense of responsibility you feel to make the world a better place. The simple chart will help you define your active interest and your awareness of issues large and small, global and local.

Ask yourself these questions:

- *Can you define what 'citizenship' means to you?*
- *Which of the following best fits your understanding? Being neighbourly? Being generous-spirited to passing human traffic each day? Being courteous – a careful driver or a considerate customer? Or is it broader? Putting coins in a charity box? Buying a copy of the* Big Issue? *Supporting a local community appeal? Or is it bigger still? Recycling as much waste as you can? Buying fair-trade food? Making sure you are informed about world affairs and that you articulate your concerned view when opportunities arise?*
- *Are you a campaigner?*
- *Do you wish you were?*
- *Specify exactly what your contribution is to making the world a better place.*

These are *big* questions! I know how you may be feeling – just writing them makes me want to crawl back under the duvet. How few of us can answer or address any of those questions without being found wanting! Amongst Life Auditors, though, citizenship has always been a recurring theme that people did want to address – especially people who seemed to have it all or who were particularly successful.

Toby, a successful copywriter, said he found his social conscience pricking so much that it made him question his well-paid lifestyle. 'It just felt wrong to go on great holidays in five-star hotels right next to a shanty town where kids had no shoes and begged outside the reception lobby. I'm not sure what I can do about it, though. It almost seems too easy just to give money to charity.' Journalist Lisa was keen to find more time in her life to use her press and publicity skills to raise funds for the local branch of a charity that supports people with multiple sclerosis. 'My dad was thought to have the disease, and I would like to get really positively involved if I had the time.'

Fundamentally, this Stocktake of your level of citizenship is all about how much time you give to others at any level. Don't be humbled if currently the only contributions you make are confined to a close circle of friends. At least now you are looking at what time you do have, and whether there is something you could do or want to do that would make a difference to someone else.

FILLING IN YOUR CITIZENSHIP STOCKTAKE

- *See chart 22.*
- *Taking the information from your Day Journals and Daily Time Logs, list the activities you participated in*

that were focused on other people beyond your own family and their needs.

- *If these took up specific time, account for it, but remember not to double account.*
- *Identify the scale and the nature of your concerns and awareness, i.e. local, national, global. This should enable you to work out whether you're interested in local politics, say, or global environmentalism.*
- *Finally, come up with a statement that defines your attitude to citizenship responsibilities.*

Soul Stocktake

What do I mean by 'soul', and how on earth can you stocktake it? I suppose I mean your spirituality, your core sense of being, your place in time. It may very well be something you don't want to consider at all, let alone tick boxes about. But then again, it might be the trigger that's propelled you into this process. If you are auditing your life because you are trying to work out what to do with it in the bigger sense, you may well have found your-self thinking hard about your inner soul. Making space in life means there is space to think more about the person you really are.

These days most of us in the developed world don't have to worry about the business of actual survival, which might crowd out thoughts of the deeper person. But, now that we have greater affluence, more choices and a whole range of ways to purchase solutions to problems, we find ourselves hankering after a better understanding of those things we can't buy the answers to. If this describes you, include contemplation of your soul in your total Stocktake.

Don't be self-conscious about considering your soul, because it's an enormously important element in your make-up. Your soul is your humanity, your brand, your unique selling point. It's defined by lots of different aspects of you. It's the part beyond your physicality – the spiritual you, the emotional you, the thinking you, the sexual you. It's what makes you the person you are. And for every one of us it's something different. Seventy-year-old Marjorie told me that, for her, 'soul' was what her father used to describe as being 'true'. Dave, 49 and just out of long service in the army, stated that it was having 'bottom'. Colette and Declan's interpretation was quite different and straightforward, with, as for a number of Life Auditors, religious connotations: 'The soul is what continues after you die.'

But how to stocktake it? Acknowledging it's there, in whatever shape, is a start. The form on which to write it all down is very simple, and is designed to prompt some thoughts to help you define what you as an individual mean by your soul.

Ask yourself these questions:

- *Do you wonder why you are here?*
- *Do you question what makes you you?*
- *Are you aware of having an inner spirit?*
- *Do you feel there is a hole in your life?*
- *Do you have religious beliefs?*
- *If so, do you question your religious beliefs?*
- *Do you need to join with others for worship?*
- *Do you have moments of deep and personal contemplation?*
- *Do you feel you want or need a spiritual guide?*

- *Do you ever experience moments of intense joy or sadness that seem to come from nowhere?*
- *Do you ever feel surprised or fearful at the strength of your emotions or desires?*
- *Do you wonder what life is all about?*
- *Do you seek a purpose in life?*
- *Are you comfortable, happy or unhappy with your sexuality?*
- *If your eyes really were the windows of your soul and someone was to look into them, what would they see?*

Be gentle with yourself and just write down words that you think describe your inner man or woman. Look at those words and 'feel' how true they are about *your* soul.

A few Life Auditors have been, at least in public, coy when it came to considering their soul. They didn't see a place for it in a down-to-earth analysis of the here and now such as the Audit. So does it matter if you skip this section? It won't affect the rest of the Audit process – but isn't what you are doing really hard-core soul-searching? So the soul would seem to have a place.

FILLING IN YOUR SOUL STOCKTAKE

- *See chart 23*
- *Treat the horizontal lines as sliding scales.*
- *Mark where you would position yourself along each line.*
- *Use the blank boxes to enter any other criteria you consider important.*
- *Assess what contribution your sexuality does or does not make to your sense of soul.*

> - *Refer back to your Daily Time Logs and consider and enter how much dedicated time you commit to your spirituality and soul in terms of such things as prayer, church-going, worship or spiritual experiences.*
> - *Write a defining statement describing your soul, making each word important.*

Mortality Stocktake

You've faced up to your soul – and there's that lobby that says it's the part of you that travels on to the other side – so to consider the question of mortality seems the logical next step. If you are facing up to your life, you must face up to your death too. This final consideration in the Stocktake section is geared to clarifying your attitude to your own mortality and giving you a chance to confront any fears or morbid worries. On a practical level, it also aims to establish what 'housekeeping' you need to do regarding your affairs and wishes in the event of your death.

It's the one certainty we have in life – the only thing we don't know is *when*. Depending on your outlook, you may be glad about that – but spare a second to consider it and to make sure, first, that your affairs are in order and, second, that should you be knocked over by a bus tomorrow you have left as little unfinished 'big' business as possible.

Ask yourself these questions:

- *Are you terrified by the prospect of death?*
- *How often do you think about it?*
- *Do you think about the process of dying or death itself?*
- *Are your affairs in order?*
- *Do you talk to your family about your wishes in the event of your death?*
- *Are you anxious about how they will cope without you?*
- *Do you feel obsessively fearful about how much of your natural span is left to you?*
- *Or do you resolutely try not to think about it, while feeling a secret dread every time you get a sense of your own mortality?*

Marjorie said she didn't fear death because her strong religious faith had prepared her for it. She was, however, anxious that her health might break down as she got older – in particular she was worried about senility or becoming incapacitated. Tom and several other hobby gardeners talked of feeling depressed with the passing of yet another growing season – that it was one less remaining to them. Gardening featured in many older people's lives, and one couple said that the planting and nurturing of seeds and cuttings each year was almost a defiant protest against the passing of time.

Fred took pride in, and comfort from, the level of organisation of his affairs. 'My daughter knows exactly where to find the file with all my instructions and paperwork – it's in the filing cabinet under D for Death!' Betty, on the other hand, was not alone in refusing point-blank to talk about death. 'Sorry, life's too short to spend worrying about not having it,' was her brisk and only response.

Either way, it's the one fact of life we all share, and that's why the Audit suggests you address it and get your thoughts about it straight. Do so if for no other reason than to make sure your affairs are in order and your next of kin are aware of your wishes – even if it's just that you have none! The confrontation of any fear you might have shouldn't increase that fear. Confrontation should in fact acknowledge it and help you come to terms with it. Further down the line your mortality might be something that you need to try to find a special comfort level to deal with. But the first stage, in this Stocktake, is to articulate to yourself how you feel about the inevitable.

FILLING IN YOUR MORTALITY STOCKTAKE

- *See chart 24.*
- *The horizontal lines represent the two extremes of attitude.*
- *Mark in the appropriate place along the line where you gauge your position to be on each issue.*
- *Write a defining statement about how you view your mortality.*

Wrapping up the First Stage of the Audit

Y ou have now addressed all the life areas suggested in this book. If there is some part of you that you don't feel you've taken account of, create your own stocktaking sheet for it. This can take the shape of simple statements or questions with a sequence of tick and cross boxes – anything that prompts an examination of the way you feel about whatever it is and the role it plays in your overall life.

If you don't know where to start, begin by jotting down random thoughts or assumptions and try to order them into plus points or minuses. Look hard at the sentences you write to see whether a common theme appears. Ask yourself what, in an ideal world, might be an answer to the problem. Interrogate yourself as though you were another person. You need to find out all you can about the issue being addressed.

That, finally, is the first stage completed, and you should now have filled in all the charts with the required information. Who'd have thought there would be so much to say about a single individual? You should be feeling a sense of achievement now that you have collated so much detailed information about yourself and are in such a strong position to start making decisions about your life and to change it if that's what you want. Well done! Despite possibly feeling 'time-poor', you have found the time to get to this point.

I expect you have seen some subtle changes in the way you deal with people and situations. Your awareness and use of time will probably be getting smarter, too, and you should now be keen to start filling the spare minutes with actions and activities related to the dreams and plans you wrote down at the very beginning.

The whole purpose of the first stage of the Audit has been to get you to this moment – the moment when your life in its entirety is spread out before you, itemised and annotated and ready for a reckoning. From the big issues to the little irritations the stuff of your life has been painstakingly accounted for, and you are now in an informed position to start the proactive job of making your life what you want it to be.

THE
life ⏱
audit

second
stage

Opening Stock – so this is who you really are

You are now very close to the moment of finding out what magic figure is going to equate with the 'Z factor' of that time equation first mentioned on page 2: the figure that tells you how much available, controllable free time you have. The Time Logs and Stocktakes should have given you a clearer idea of all the components of your life that need your attention, and will also have helped define the real you. By establishing who you really are, you have calculated the 'Y factor' – the time taken up by definite needs, commitments and non-negotiables.

You can calculate Z on a daily or weekly basis, but, to demonstrate the scale of the opportunity you have, aim to take the exercise on to cover a whole year. As explained before, this entails calculating typical events and commitments across the number of average *working* days and *non-working* days over the course of a year. You have already worked these out as you considered each of your life areas, and now you need only look at the bottom line time totals and transfer them to the next document, your Balance Sheet.

Adding together all your committed time will allow you to calculate your total. Now subtract that total from the number of hours in whatever period of time you are auditing, and Z is the figure remaining. That is the disposable time you have to spend, fritter away, add value to an aspect of your life or invest in realising a dream.

FILLING IN YOUR BALANCE SHEET

- *See chart 25.*
- *Enter the total number of hours available (X) i.e. in the Audit period/the whole year.*
- *Go back over your Stocktake sheets and add up the time commitments you have calculated in each life area.*
- *Enter your life areas down the left-hand side of the sheet, with the corresponding time totals for your Audit period.*
- *Add together to reach a grand total of hours committed (Y).*
- *Subtract this figure from the number of hours in the period you are assessing (X).*
- *The remainder is the number of hours you have free (Z).*
- *Some quick multiplication will allow you to arrive at a figure for the year as a whole.*

Breakeven – do just this and survive

So there you have it: the time that is really and truly yours for the taking. Your Stocktake of yourself is an analysis of how you spend your time and some straightforward situation reports on the way you feel about the life issues that concern you. That's you stocktaken! I wonder how you feel as you look at it. Astonished, fazed, pleased? What you are seeing is the reality of your life today. You may have already made some changes along the way, and this is just the beginning.

You should feel that the figure you have just calculated, which represents your currently uncommitted hours, is like suddenly coming across a forgotten building society account or getting a tax rebate. You had a feeling it was there, but seeing it as a figure on a sheet of paper makes it real. This Audit is all about finding out that figure and then doing something with it. But before you move on to that stage you need to see if you can increase that figure – because, after all, you reached it by looking piecemeal at your *current* lifestyle. Now you are in a much better informed position and should have a much more realistic and pragmatic overview of your day-to-day life and obligations. Maybe you were disappointed that you don't appear to have more spare time. So before you move on you need to consider if you can crank even more value out of your waking hours and improve that bottom line Breakeven figure.

The aim of this section, therefore, is to maximise the time you have free to do what you want by saving even more time on duties and compulsory tasks. The assumption being made here is that for most of us the headings we've chosen are 'must-dos', 'must-haves' or 'should-think abouts'. If we can find a succinct and streamlined approach to each of them, so that they are dealt with in a time-efficient way and receive from us only what they need and deserve and no more, then we can start to add extra value to the rest of life and pursue some of our dreams.

Take from my experiences and those of other previous Life Auditors anything that will help you. Remember, there is no single right way to reach the sort of personal equilibrium you are hoping to achieve. Whatever works for you is great – if none of the time-saving tips or advice relates to your life, try to find your own ways to reach a realistic Breakeven position that will be the firm base from which to leap forward in the third stage.

Revisit your original Stocktake forms to make adjustments. As with everything else, you can choose the order in which you address things – I'm continuing the order established in the first stage and following the way my own use of time happened.

Sleep Breakeven

During your stocktaking period you should have worked out the average number of hours' sleep you need each night and established whether you are a lark or an owl. These things are crucial in determining both the time you go to bed and how you feel when you wake up. The point of this section is to see whether you can maximise the benefit of however many hours' sleep you are getting, and also to check that overall there is definitely no room for reduction. Many people think they are as sleep-starved as they are time-poor. But time and again Life Auditors have reported that, once into the Audit process, they changed the pattern of their sleep and in almost all cases this meant a reduction.

Until my mid-twenties I was an owl and had to force myself to go to bed, even in the early hours of the morning. I could and did sleep in until late morning whenever I could. Then two things happened: I had my first child and I started working on breakfast television. This meant that I got into the habit of grabbing sleep whenever I could and developed a spectacular ability to cat-nap, including, memorably, at restaurant tables and while waiting in the car at traffic lights. With the children

Second Stage

131

now grown up and my 3a.m. starts behind me, my routine has stayed that of a lark – and I have to say that, in terms of time-saving, it comes highly recommended.

For me, the most valuable hours of each day are between five and eight each morning. I seem to be able to get three times as much done then as at any other time of day. There are practical reasons for that. Once I'm fully awake I'm at my freshest, and there are no distractions in terms of phones or other people. The house is quiet, I'm not tempted to slump in front of the TV, and in fact by the time the working day proper starts I'm raring to go, with my thoughts and everything else well ordered.

Ask yourself these questions:

- *Do you have a regular bedtime?*
- *Do you have a routine you always follow at bedtime?*
- *Is the amount of sleep you get critical?*
- *Do you feel rested when you wake?*
- *Is your sleep tranquil or troubled?*
- *Do you often dream?*
- *Does your waking time allow enough measured time to prepare you for the day ahead?*

Set your alarm for an hour earlier than normal and see how much more you get done and how much more prepared you are for the day ahead. One effect of this is that you may need to head off for bed a little earlier, too. In most cases, though, unless you really are a committed owl you will probably find that your body clock quickly adjusts to its new start time. One of the most common time-gaining actions that Life Auditors reported was getting up earlier in the morning, and I've talked to enough people who are happy with six or even five hours a night to know that there are many exceptions to that eight-hour average.

So, if you are currently committed to eight hours it's worth seeing if you can get away with less. You can always catch up at weekends or on holiday. Or maybe you will be able to identify another piece of usable time – having a nap in the car at lunchtime and paying back some of your sleep debt might be better for you than eating, shopping or chatting to colleagues. But be sensible: if, for instance, you drive a lot or operate machinery, you and others could be at risk if you become drowsy through lack of sleep. So if this describes you, be extra-careful about cutting down your night-time kip.

The quality of your sleep is important, too. For me, a troubled night is the first indicator of some underlying concern or stress. Although it's the first use of time you may decide to pare down, it's vital that you get good-quality sleep and as much of it as you need to function.

Ask yourself these questions:

- *Is your bed comfortable?*
- *Is your bedroom a peaceful, sleep-inducing sanctuary?*
- *What elements distract you from sleep?*
- *What elements enhance sleep?*
- *Are the temperature and ventilation right?*
- *Are there any routines or habits that help you to sleep?*

My own answers to these questions gave rise to a number of actions. I removed my desk from the bedroom. (It had been the quietest place to work, but having the computer in the corner of the room didn't encourage drowsiness.) I decided to save up for a new mattress. I bought a radio that could be push-button selected to BBC World Service

Second Stage

and Radio Four and then easily switched back to Radio Two in the morning, a good supply of lavender-scented candles and pot-pourri, brighter bedside lights. And, bizarrely, I started ironing my duvet covers for the first time in my life. Duvet cover ironing is a classic case of conceding to give more time to one aspect of life in order to reap greater advantage in another, because on balance the added value to me outweighed the loss of time.

Duvet cover ironing, rather like drying up hand-washed plates that can be stacked in a drainer, had always seemed a ludicrous waste of time. Apart from being an unwieldy thing to iron and fold, a duvet cover gets creased and crumpled within seconds of use – and in any case who's to know you haven't bothered when it's then hidden under a bedcover? Annoyingly, however, I discovered that I fall asleep like a baby when I slide between smooth ironed linen. So I had to accept it was time well spent.

It took me a long time to realise how soothing it was if my bedroom actually *looked* more like the sanctuary it should be. Whatever your sleep requirements, make your bed and bedroom a safe retreat where you can be comfortable and rested even when you are not fast asleep.

WAYS TO IMPROVE YOUR SLEEP BREAKEVEN

- *Try to reduce the amount of sleep you have by one hour, and see how you feel.*
- *Note where and how often you need to compensate for the above by repaying any sleep debt.*
- *Make your bedroom a suitable sanctuary for sleep.*

- *Buy blackout blinds or line your curtains with blackout material.*
- *Experiment with different levels of heating and ventilation.*
- *Establish a calming routine in the run-up to going to bed.*

A final word on sleep and the time it takes up. Unless you are a chronic insomniac and sleeplessness is adversely affecting your life, try to be relaxed about those nights when you toss and turn and can't achieve any shut-eye. If it's three in the morning, you are the only person awake in the household and you've tried all the old chestnuts such as counting sheep and making yourself a milky drink, stop worrying about how tired you are going to feel in the morning. Instead, consider this time a real gift and use it to get on with something that was going to have to be done during the day. Either tick off some chores and 'must-dos' from your list or, once you've got further along the Audit chain, view the time as an investment opportunity to start progressing a plan or ambition by reading up on a subject or making notes. The chances are that once you start to do something you'll feel overcome with drowsiness and will want to go back to sleep. If not, you'll have used the time cleverly. Either way – win, win!

Health Breakeven

The stocktaking you did on your health and the statement you came up with about how healthy and fit you are make up a performance report based on information from your

Day Journal. The Stocktake will have provided you with a current Breakeven position of the time and commitment it takes to stay healthy. You have considered your physical wellbeing, fitness and diet, and now you are simply going to look at your bottom line commitment to see if you can improve the situation. You will be doing this in terms of the amount of time that looking after your health, fitness and weight takes up, and also to make sure that you are getting the best value out of the effort and energy you put into this important part of your life.

You should be able to come up with an overall picture of the current time demands that being healthy (or not being healthy) and keeping healthy make upon your days; these demands will range from incapacitation to regular check-ups or personal routines. You will also have a better understanding of any trigger situations or environments that prompt health problems. Finally, any mismatch between your health and the demands you make on your body will be crystal-clear. That Breakeven position should make your health and its management a no stress, efficiently executed responsibility.

Be cheered by the fact that just doing the Life Audit has probably improved your health. Stress and anxiety can be manifested in many physical conditions from raised blood pressure to heart disease, depression and dependency on alcohol, cigarettes or drugs. One cause of stress is having to cope with uncertainty and disorder. The Life Audit's emphasis on facing reality and bringing routine and order into your life should be helping already if you suffer from stress.

Although the Audit is about *self*-assessment, you do occasionally need to involve outside professionals in areas that require specialist knowledge. Health is one such area, and people such as your doctor, dentist and optician are the professionals. If you are, on the whole, quite healthy you probably won't have paid them much thought. However, should you need medical support or advice these hitherto anonymous practitioners will become individuals to whom you are having to entrust your wellbeing and maybe even your life.

At this Breakeven stage, really consider the relationships you have with your health professionals. You are going to make sure each of them has all the right strengths and qualities *now*, before they ever have to be tested.

Ask yourself these questions:

- *Do you trust each of your current health professionals?*
- *Do you like them?*
- *Are you able to talk to them easily, however intimate the problem?*
- *Do you know all you need to know about them?*
- *What is the extent of the care they can offer?*
- *Have they any specialist experience?*
- *What clinics, screening or check-ups are available?*
- *How frequently should you have check-ups?*

If you don't immediately know the answers to any of the above, contact the relevant health professionals, ask the relevant questions and find out what services you are eligible for. Double-check the frequency of examinations and check-ups you might need to have, and book yourself appointments at the appropriate time.

If you can, make all your regular health appointments for the same day, or over a short group of days, and plot them into your diary to form a specific time 'island' in which your health issues are prioritised rather than sidelined for consideration as and when things go wrong.

Second Stage

If your Health Audit has thrown up any concerns, or if an existing ailment, however minor, has been troubling you, make an appointment with the doctor, dentist or optician. Since you are now armed with a close catalogue of how the problem affects your day-to-day living, you will be able to furnish the relevant medical expert with all they need to know to help you get well again, or at the very least to 'manage' the condition.

Ask yourself these questions:

- *Do you want to look into the possibility of a different or alternative remedy?*
- *Do you want to investigate any medication you are on, in order to be better aware of possible side-effects or long-term issues?*
- *Do you wish to clarify what ongoing supervision your problem might need?*

The Appointment Notes chart will help you collate the information you need to have ready. Given that most medical professionals work to a tight time-to-patient ratio, it will ensure that you make the absolute most of the time you have with them.

FILLING IN YOUR APPOINTMENT NOTES FORM

- *See chart 26.*
- *Record your main symptoms, including any unusual aches, pains or twinges even if they seem unrelated.*
- *State the time period over which you have been*

The Life Audit

138

recording the symptoms.

- *Mention any situations or circumstances that could have been triggers for the condition.*
- *Draw attention to any relevant medical history that might have a bearing on the diagnosis.*
- *Enter any medication you are currently on or have been prescribed in the past for the condition.*
- *If you are interested in any alternative treatments, enter them in the appropriate space as a reminder to ask about them.*
- *Add any information you have gleaned through your own research. This might be about new treatments or possible side-effects.*
- *Finally, use the Notes box to jot things down during the consultation, in case you suffer from appointment amnesia. Remember that, as well as seeking a solution to your problem, you are also making sure you receive the right treatment to enable you to manage the problem most effectively.*

The appointment is also an invaluable opportunity to take a closer look at the health professional. This is the time to ask yourself all those questions about how well you know them, and how well suited they are to you and to your current and possible future health needs. Tell them that you have been paying close attention to your health and intend to be more aware of it from now on. Judge how they respond to that news, and consider how helpful and supportive they are likely to be if you need to seek their advice in the future rather than just needing their services

Second Stage

in an emergency. This meeting is more than just an appointment to 'fix' a broken bit of you – it's an opportunity to put some effort into what may one day be a vital relationship. Optimise it by having useful information and a list of questions at the ready.

While there, get a second opinion on any assumptions you've made about yourself – about matters such as diet and fitness. Talk, too, about any bad habits you want to address, such as smoking, and find out what support may be on offer. Find out about specialist clinics, which might include asthma, diabetes, fertility, menopause and breast health. The practice nurse may also offer a full range of health checks including blood pressure, cholesterol and cervical smears. Ask if you are eligible for these and at what frequency you should have them. Make sure that you are carrying out any DIY checks properly. You know your body better than anyone else, and are best placed to spot any warning signs. You should check your breasts or testicles regularly for any lumps or bumps – if you are not sure you are doing it right, now is the time to ask.

If you are concerned about any possible inherited conditions, talk about them at this appointment; there may be some specialist screening that could put your mind at rest. Make sure you have the correct spelling of any condition or diagnosis so that you can take responsibility for understanding it better by doing some research into it, which should cover any appropriate self-help procedures and alternative treatment options.

The consultation with your doctor (and, indeed, with your dentist and optician) while you are conducting the Life Audit is likely to have a bearing on the time any health issue takes in your life, and should allow for some time shifts and demands that will give you a truer and more economic Breakeven position on your health. See if you can improve your Breakeven position so that looking after your health takes up less time and causes the least amount of concern.

WAYS TO IMPROVE YOUR HEALTH BREAKEVEN

- *Really get to know your health professionals.*
- *Be informed about the healthcare provision available to you.*
- *Be methodical, and stay up-to-date with check-ups and routine screening.*
- *Take responsibility for understanding your condition.*
- *Make DIY health checks part of your personal routine.*
- *Optimise appointment time with health professionals.*
- *As you get older, respond to health concerns promptly by seeking advice, and be wise about preventive measures such as flu jabs.*
- *Try to get early appointment times in surgery or clinic sessions to avoid accumulated appointment over-runs.*

Fitness Breakeven

Fitness should have been a particular, tangible aspect of your health to account for in the Time Logs. However, the Breakeven point you set may change constantly as you continue to adjust the fitness demands you make on yourself. Judging by the reports of most Life Auditors, fitness is an area that sees an immediate injection of extra time and effort. So be happy to make ongoing adjustments to your Breakeven level. Now you need to submit it to

Second Stage

further scrutiny to see if it can be improved upon and whether the exercise you get is currently taking the most effective and efficient form.

Don't let your age limit your fitness expectations. Being fit will help you live life at an optimum pitch, stay mobile and actually help you to avoid some of the health problems that come with ageing. Seventy-year-old Alan said he had made himself be very disciplined about keeping fit. 'When I retired it would have been very easy to slip into watching a lot of daytime TV and becoming quite inactive. I have a rigid routine that involves me being active that I don't let myself veer away from. For instance, whatever the weather, or how I feel, I walk the mile to the shops and back each morning to get my newspaper. I could have it delivered or take the car, but I've all the time in the world and the exercise helps keep me fit.'

Being fitter will also benefit all other areas in the Life Audit. Government advice recommends 20 minutes of exercise three times a week. Exercise will help you relax, improve your strength, keep your heart healthy, give you energy, help you to lose weight, and if undertaken as a group activity or sport it can be mentally stimulating and help you to meet people. You will also have identified areas in your life which aren't specific exercise or designed as fitness regimes but that are examples of activity that make a contribution to your overall fitness.

Ask yourself these questions:

- *Do you think the exercise you get is adequate to achieve the fitness level you have set yourself?*
- *Have you explored other exercise or fitness regimes to see if they might be as effective and enjoyable and take*

less time?

- *Is there scope to raise your game in your chosen exercise, and so to get more benefit out of less time?*
- *Does the exercise you get efficiently burn off any excess calories you consume?*

The Fitness Planner should help you organise your fitness routine efficiently and ensure you introduce variety and balance.

FILLING IN YOUR FITNESS PLANNER

- *See chart 27.*
- *It's split into a.m. and p.m. for seven days.*
- *Enter the type of exercise, e.g. running, walking, cross training.*
- *Enter the intensity, e.g. moderate, brisk.*
- *Enter the amount of time you plan to exercise.*
- *The additional line is to record any other data you need to make a note of.*

Whatever your action plan for your fitness, you may find it worthwhile to consider the following tips.

WAYS TO IMPROVE YOUR FITNESS BREAKEVEN

- *Talk to an expert in your chosen fitness routine to see if they can give you professional advice about how you could get more out of less time.*
- *Ask your doctor if he operates a Fitness on Prescription scheme that will help you discover which type of activity is best suited to your fitness needs.*
- *Are any of your friends or family interested in the same activity? If so, could you combine socialising time with fitness time?*
- *Along the same lines, develop new habits and, instead of meeting friends for lunch or a drink, suggest a walk instead.*
- *Could your fitness routine be done in the hour you plan to steal from your sleep?*
- *If your fitness regime involves going out to a gym or to play sport with others, also have a private routine that you can work out to at home on days when time allocated to exercise gets unavoidably reduced.*
- *Seize all your 'lifestyle' fitness opportunities. Do everything a little faster. Jog on the spot while you are waiting for the kettle to boil. Do squats when you are picking up laundry from the kids' bedroom floor. Make big sweeps with your arms when you are washing the car or cleaning windows. Put a dance track on while you are vacuuming.*

Weight and Diet Breakeven

Your diet is evidence of your relationship with food, and only you will know whether a change in your eating habits might produce a different Breakeven level from the one you have reached so far in your Audit, and whether that in turn might yield lifestyle or time benefits. My personal gluttony was very time-consuming, as the scales demonstrated each morning. My Audit revealed just how food-obsessed I was – I was amazed when I did the calculation that combined the amount of time I devoted to thinking about it, looking at recipes and shopping for different ingredients, let alone the actual cooking and eating. It was obvious that if I could devote less time to food not only was there time to be gained but there would also be great health dividends.

My personal management plan was to eat plain for a while – just grilled or roast meat and fish with salads. That immediately eliminated the need to pore over cookery books or recipes and a lot of finicky preparation of ingredients. It also cut down on shopping time and clearing away, too. But because cooking is also for me a hobby and a creative pleasure I knew I couldn't give it up completely, so I decided to get my fix at the stove by concentrating on preserves and cakes (which my lack of sweet tooth meant I wouldn't eat and which I gave to family and friends). It worked for me, and if your own relationship with food needs attention from either a time or health standpoint, you too need to do a bit of lateral and creative thinking to find a happy balance.

Ask yourself these questions:

- *Do you eat to live, or live to eat?*
- *Do you think about food often during the day?*
- *Are those thoughts confined to moments when you feel hungry? Or do you enjoy anticipating the different meals and tastes you want to try?*
- *Do you feel guilty about how much you eat?*
- *If you only ate what your body needed nutritionally you wouldn't be overweight, so is food a substitute for something else lacking in your life?*
- *Are you kidding yourself that you are happy with your weight?*
- *Are you confident you are eating a healthy, balanced diet?*
- *Are there trigger situations that make you reach for the biscuit tin?*

The Meal Planner chart should be useful in bringing order to your own and your family's eating habits, even if you aren't watching what you eat. It shouldn't mean you have a less imaginative or delicious diet, but should be the manifestation of all these good intentions you are committing to as part of your planned Breakeven position.

FILLING IN YOUR MEAL PLANNER

- *See chart 28.*
- *Itemise what each meal in the coming week will consist of.*
- *Check you have built in variety and have selected menus you will look forward to.*
- *Make sure the preparation required by any particular*

meal is achievable, given that day's other events and time commitments.

- *If you want to monitor your diet, the two small boxes in each meal space are for you to fill in the dietary units of the meal. These can be whatever you choose – calories, carbohydrates, fat grams, diet plan points or units. Enter your planned intake in one box and your actual intake in the other. Remember that, if you are cooking for, say, a family of four, you will only need to record your own share of the meal.*

The section on home and domestic duties contains more tips on how to cut back on time when buying and storing food, but meanwhile here are a few ideas that can save time while enabling you to follow healthy diet principles.

WAYS TO IMPROVE YOUR WEIGHT AND DIET BREAKEVEN

- *Save time cooking and maximise your nutrient intake by eating vegetables and fruit raw whenever you can.*
- *Cook vegetables and fruit such as potatoes and apples in their skins to save time and maximise the amount of goodness you get.*
- *Find taste in what you cook, not how you cook, by buying good-quality meat and fish and serving them simply roast or grilled.*
- *Stir-frying is another healthy, speedy way to cook.*
- *Consider consulting a nutritionist or buying a book to*

> learn how your body processes food.
> - Plan a week's menus and shop for it all at once (use the compartmentalised Shopping List, chart 30, to keep your food thoughts limited to necessities). Apart from saving time, if the right food is already bought and in the fridge you are less likely to indulge on impulse.
> - Only serve fruit, cheese or good yogurts for pudding.
> - Listen to your inner man or woman, and only sit down to eat when you're hungry.
> - Stop eating when you're no longer hungry.
> - If you're dieting, always have the next meal virtually ready to eat so that you have no excuses for grabbing quick-fix calories.

Relationship Breakeven

Stocktaking your relationships should have resulted in a definitive list of the people in your life and the amount of time they take up. You have probably found your relationships challenging to audit and it's this next exercise, aimed at finding the Breakeven needs of any personal connection, that may tax you the most.

You have put together an all-encompassing list of people in a range of categories from partners to support services and professionals. Each will have an amount of dedicated 'time need' next to it; by 'dedicated' I mean the special time you make to be with that person or those people. Added up, all that time is your current Relationship Breakeven.

Other Breakeven sections contain specific practical advice on how to save time and cut corners – there are plenty of tips, for instance, on how to make housework or wardrobe choices time-efficient so as to free up extra minutes that can be used for something more positive and proactive. However, relationships are too personal and unique to each of us to be treated in this way by anyone but the person doing the Audit on themselves. Only you know whether short-cut measures where relationships are concerned will leave your conscience pricking and so defeat the point of the Audit exercise.

Relationships are, in my opinion, the most important time investments we all make, and that's why their time requirements need to be established at an early stage in the Breakeven equation. Other life demands can then fit in around them. So this part of the Breakeven section doesn't offer clever ruses or suggest priorities. What it will do is help you achieve clarity about who you want to spend time with and who you don't, and it also offers advice on adding value or improving the quality of your associations.

Significant others

You should be crystal-clear about the people at the very centre of your life. So, starting with your core relationships – your partner, children, maybe your parents or even your pet – you should know already whether they are getting the share of your life and attention that they deserve and that you want to devote to them. If they aren't, adjust the time entry. You should find the time!

Of course, what the Audit may have thrown up, or what you may have known already, is that one of your core or very close relationships is a source of distress or is malfunctioning. If so, what you need to do right now is find the happiest balance you can: the aim is to satisfy yourself and the person you are having the relationship with that you are measuring your time as best you can and that the relationship, however troubled, has been given priority. Your desire to address any area of unhappiness in any important relationship should appear on your Relationship auditor's statement and also in your Really Personal Information. So if there are communication problems, jealousies, rivalries or a falling out of love, write it in as an issue that needs, and will get, major consideration further along the Audit journey. But in the meantime let's get back to making sure you are giving quality time, and enough of it, to your most important relationships.

Ask yourself these questions:

- *What time and energy do you want to give your close relationships? Is there currently a shortfall?*
- *Are the people in your very close relationships quite forgiving and tolerant of shortfalls if they don't get their fair share of time?*
- *If so, are you abusing that tolerance?*
- *Is life so full with work commitments and other friends and wider family duties that you never have enough time to dedicate to special relationships?*
- *Is there a danger of any of your special relationships lapsing into purely a practical or financial arrangement if you don't find time to make more of an effort?*
- *What sort of 'dedicated' time would you and the other person involved appreciate?*

For your Core Relationships Breakeven you should think 'ideal world' in terms of time, and consider what you and they would really benefit from. With your partner, perhaps that's a regular evening in together each week with a video and a takeaway, a twice-yearly 'special' holiday break, or just more time on a day-to-day basis. With the kids, is it being at home for them at breakfast or bathtime, doing the school run regularly, or being on the touchline to watch the mid-week match? With your parents, perhaps it's regular phone calls and pre-planned visits or outings. At this stage, you are trying to determine what sort of activity would be good and you don't need to decide specifically what you are doing with the time you are putting aside – just make sure it's there. If, though, you find an enormous mismatch between your ideal Breakeven position and what you realistically know you are going to be able to achieve within your current situation, you must transfer the consideration of this relationship to your Really Personal Information sheet.

For instance, if I had done the Audit at one stage in my mid-thirties, I'd have had to put down that I wanted to give up work and be a full-time mother. That would have been impractical and improbable without other far-reaching life changes, so it would have had to be entered as a wish that needed to be considered when I looked at my life in the round further along the way.

Sally, mother of three children aged twelve, nine and seven, and with a full-time office job, decided the only way to stay close and keep her relationship special with her husband Peter was to treat it like a business relationship and fix weekly appointments when they could be alone together. 'It became part of our Sunday evening routine to look at the diary for the coming week and put in a time and date to see each other. Otherwise *our* time would always have been taken over and become other people's.'

Mark and Louise had only been married a couple of years but both felt their relationship had lost its spark. Mark said he actually felt quite lonely in the marriage. 'We sat down and really studied what we'd done together in the past week, and that made it clear that we were falling into a rut of eating supper in front of the TV every night and going off doing separate things at the weekend. Louise would go shopping, while I'd watch sport with my mates. We didn't spend *any* time talking or doing things together outside home. We'd forgotten how we used to enjoy doing stuff when we first met.'

WAYS TO IMPROVE YOUR CORE RELATIONSHIP BREAKEVEN

- *Ensure you make time to be together.*
- *Use that time to engage with each other properly, e.g. don't eat while watching TV but use the time to talk.*
- *If it's your partner, remember the things that attracted you to each other in the first place.*
- *Remind yourself that you have placed this individual, whether partner, child, parent, best friend or pet, at the centre of your life. These are your most important relationships.*
- *Accept that you have a responsibility with regard to core relationships.*
- *Don't ignore others' needs in working out your own. You are an interdependent unit.*
- *Don't only hear, really listen to what is being said. Even arguments can be full of information.*

> • *If you are spending time railing against some injustice or imbalance in the relationship, address it openly. After all, you have identified this relationship as too important to get wrong or to waste with misunderstanding. If this relationship has a significant problem, write it down and make dealing with it a priority on your Really Personal Information sheet.*

Family

Beyond your partner and children or other core relationship, think about the rest of your family. Families often have cast lists of characters – the bossy one, the joker, the eccentric, the martyr, the victim and so on. Some family members may make demands of you, for instance, or it may be that you are the needy one in the family dynamic. Whichever it is, you need to decide the Breakeven level of contact required by each of your family relationships. Look back over your Audit period – see what time you did manage to spend with family members and judge whether you would like to have committed more or less time, or whether you had it just about right. Was it dedicated quality time, or was it along-the-way time that fitted in with your life's other engagements?

Ask yourself these questions:

- *What form of contact is most practical and agreeable to you, e.g. phone call, email, visit or outing?*
- *What form of contact would be most appreciated by the other person?*
- *If there is a mismatch, can you find a compromise?*

Second Stage

153

- *What is the minimum frequency of contact you want to commit to?*
- *If you had more spare time, would you devote more to family members rather than to doing something else?*

Think 'ideal world' again and put against a list of family names a revised (if necessary) minimum level of contact you and they would be comfortable with. It may be a weekly phone call, Sunday tea, a lunchtime drink in the pub with a sibling, or an occasional note or email to a great-aunt. Don't be sheepish about what might seem to be a clinical approach to familial love and obligation. This is a kind of insurance process that is going to make sure you *do* fulfil your commitment to family members. Your relationship with them is coming high in your time demands list, and deciding upon the minimum time they need doesn't mean you can't or won't give more – it just makes sure it doesn't get missed out when other pressing demands are made upon you.

WAYS TO IMPROVE YOUR FAMILY RELATIONSHIP BREAKEVEN

- *As well as thinking about your own idea of the Breakeven, consider what individual family members might like. A frequent email or phone call might be more appreciated than the once-a-year duty visit.*
- *Work out what sort of contact best reinforces and demonstrates the level of love and support in the relationship.*
- *Try to erase 'duty' contact by finding a way to be more*

concerned with and engaged by the person in question.

- *Remind yourself why you feel an obligation to stay in contact with a particular member of the family.*
- *Do they feel a mutual duty to maintain relations?*
- *If so, can you encourage them to share the initiative?*
- *If you can't erase a 'duty' element, be strict with yourself about fulfilling the duty calls or contact on a regular and pragmatic basis. Don't let guilt creep into the equation.*
- *Family relationships don't necessarily have to be one-on-one. Family gatherings can be great ways to reinforce these relationships, and a couple of them a year may be a happier option than individual occasions.*

Friends

Having, as part of the Audit process, looked at the time you spend on all the people in your life, you should have spotted any excesses or misses with friends or acquaintances. If any fall into a grey area between firm and casual friends, thoughts about how much time and what sort of effort you're prepared to give them should clarify their place in your life.

Current circumstance and geography can mean that people who are here and present are easier to see and spend time with than those who aren't. But distance shouldn't be an obstacle to establishing some level of caring contact, especially since email and phone are so quick and easy. You need to examine your friendships to decide what Breakeven level of energy and time they need and warrant. Think closely, too, about how supportive you are to each other. Can you show your vulnerability to them, and do you mind if they do the same to you?

Jack's friends were so important to him that they were more involved in his life than his family. 'There's a gang of us, all in the same boat, blokes and girls, single, thirty-somethings, all living away from our folks and we do everything together, know all about each other and support each other. I'd be more likely to ask advice, even borrow money, from my friends than my family.' At the other extreme – and this is where courage may have to be called upon – do you, in your heart of hearts, have friendships that sap your spirit and that you want to relegate to the back row or to audit out of your life completely?

Ask yourself these questions:

- *What does a particular friendship bring to your life?*
- *Is the friendship part of a wider circle of friends?*
- *Do you particularly want to nurture this friendship?*
- *Does contact with the person in question tax you or depress you?*
- *Does your heart sink when they ring?*
- *Do they bore you rigid?*
- *Would they 'be there' for you if you needed them?*
- *Do they make you feel guilty?*
- *Do they belittle you?*
- *Do you need and like to see each other in person, in a specific environment?*
- *Do you keep up with each other predominantly by phone or email?*
- *How regularly do you like to have that contact?*
- *Do you know that they care as much or as little about you as you do about them?*
- *Have you maintained contact with them through habit or politeness?*
- *When circumstances throw you together, do you assume*

the mantle of friendship despite having no core affection for them?

Neil and Ann moved to South Wales from Manchester and at first were pleased to have old friends to stay. 'But it became obvious that we didn't have as much in common with some friends as we'd thought,' said Ann, 'and to be honest, some weekends felt like a lifetime given over to people we found we also didn't even like very much, even though in short bursts before we'd had fun.' So they just stopped issuing invites to visit Wales. 'It sounds rather ruthless and I'm sure some people wondered why, but nobody ever said anything and eventually those relationships fell by the wayside. If any of them had invited themselves down we'd have made an excuse. Meeting up for a drink or something to eat when we go back to Manchester is fine, but I'm not prepared to give up a whole weekend.'

Joe and Oliver had a similar problem with their friends, even though forty years separated them. 'I sometimes feel I'm providing the cabaret,' said 61-year-old Joe. 'It's all very well being the life and soul of the party, but I get fed up with it sometimes and wonder how they'd react if one day I turned up really depressed and needed them to cheer me up.' Oliver had a similar story. 'I get fed up with always having to be the one who organises what our crowd are going to do, where we're going to meet, and doing all the ringing around. Then when we meet up, I feel everyone expects me to make sure they have a good time.'

You may, of course, have to do some balancing assessments of other issues. There will be friends you can't drop because, despite how you feel about them, they *need*

Second Stage

157

you in their life for some reason and, being a decent person, you won't fail them or refuse whatever support they require. But if that's the case, can you describe the relationship you have with them as friendship? Karen, a gregarious 60-year-old whose social energy knows no bounds and who seems to have a large number of waifs and strays in her circle, was relieved, when she did her Audit, to find she could transfer several friends and indeed some of her extended family into her citizenship reckoning. 'I'm happy to be there for them, but to be honest it's a bit of a one-way street and I can't really class them as friends who'd pull out all the stops for me.'

Then there are also those friends of friends or friends of the family. You may have nothing in common with your boyfriend's rugby chums but tolerate the weekly pre-match pub lunches because you love him. The time spent with them should be entered as time invested in your relationship with your man.

This exercise should focus your mind on the friendships you particularly want to nurture and enable you to place others, less important but still time- and energy-consuming ones, further down your mental 'need to' list.

WAYS TO IMPROVE YOUR FRIENDS BREAKEVEN

- *Determine to really treasure the time you are committing to a relationship.*
- *View your friendships as part of a stable network that has its own dependences and loyalties.*

- *Don't waste time on relationships that consistently make you feel miserable.*
- *Consider your friends as hand-picked assets and allies.*
- *If you are maintaining a friendship because either you or they are getting something out of it, and it's not based on mutual care and affection, transfer it to another category.*
- *A multi-gathering can be a good way to see less than close friends who move in a similar circle, such as former colleagues or university contemporaries, who might enjoy getting together at a party or on an arranged night out.*
- *If you are auditing a friend out of your life you don't necessarily have to do anything actively. By not fostering the relationship they may get the message, and they may even be as relieved as you.*
- *If they don't get the message and have obviously noticed you cooling off, remain resolute.*
- *Keep auditing your friendships and adjusting your expectations.*
- *If a previously valued friend lets you down and you are considering whether to audit the relationship right out of your life, allow a cooling-off period in a metaphorical sin bin to see if it's a temporary blip.*
- *If you have decided to put special effort into one relationship and have transferred that action to your Really Personal Information wish list, then you have bought yourself some time by postponing any necessary time expenditure until the next stage of the Audit.*

And finally, if you tell any of your friends what the Breakeven position is for their relationship with you,

Second Stage

159

expect to have one less relationship to worry about! At the very least prepare to be ribbed, and for every phone contact, every invite to lunch or suggestion to meet to be greeted with a barbed enquiry about whether you are ticking a box. You have been warned!

Acquaintances

Is having acquaintances out of fashion? The trend today seems to be that we become intimate with people far more quickly than in the past, and that fleeting acquaintanceship doesn't particularly seem to have a place. But the acquaintance category is very useful, and if it doesn't feature in your life I recommend you introduce it and place in it those people with whom you have polite, in passing, but mainly disinterested contact within the course of each day. It might be people you meet daily at the bus-stop and exchange pleasantries with, a fellow regular at your local pub, or another mother at the school gate. It's a great catch-all category for people with whom you have some common currency of location or event but share nothing else with beyond that.

However, that doesn't mean that any brief encounter, such as that with the gym receptionist, can't be a life-enhancing or well-poisoning moment. Smile at a complete stranger and they will probably smile back. Snap at someone who queue-jumps at the bus-stop and you'll both end up in a foul mood. So try to make every encounter, however small, pleasant rather than thoughtless. Make eye contact and start a 'smile relay' by making yours the first baton to be passed on. You can add value to the way you interact with acquaintances, but you won't be able to improve the Breakeven position because all these encounters should be incidental and therefore use negligible time.

Colleagues

This category of contact presents different relationship dilemmas. You may find that some of the people you work with can actually be termed friends. However a word of caution, which will be endorsed by anyone who has left a job fully expecting to keep in touch with the workmates they've left behind. Susan in accounts may well be the girl you've gossiped with at the water cooler for the last three years – but the minute you or she move on to new office surroundings the common currency of your work environment will be removed, and without that relationship 'glue' you may well find that you don't have very much in common.

Putting amiability aside for a minute, colleagues are people who work with you to deliver the expectations of your employer. It's as simple as that. Unless you are the boss, there won't be a lot you can do about the time you spend in their company. But it *is* worth quality controlling how much extra time investment you make in your relationships with your colleagues outside the workplace. Do consider what happens during your lunch break or immediately after work when everyone troops down to the pub. Do you really *want* to spend that free time with the people you *have* to spend the rest of the working day with, especially if you know that other relationships are feeling squeezed of time elsewhere in your life?

While you are trying to establish the Breakeven position for all your relationships you have the perfect opportunity to ask yourself about the amount of extra, incidental time you are giving people with whom you already spend a considerable amount of time. Of course, this 'down time' with your colleagues may represent an important part of your week. But just make sure you have given it serious thought now, and enter an honest Breakeven amount of time that properly reflects the needs of these relationships.

Professionals and support services

You can be much more pragmatic about your dealings with these people. They are the human face of the functional areas of your life, and if these relationships are working well, they, like those with acquantainces, should be low-maintenance, with the Breakeven of managing them too minimal to calculate or improve upon. You simply need to ask yourself whether these relationships require or in fact do take up time beyond functional necessity. If they do, is there a better Breakeven position to be found? In much the same way as you dealt with your doctor and other healthcare professionals you now need to apply critical criteria to interaction with your accountant, bank manager, cleaner, au pair, gardener and so on.

Ask yourself these questions:

- *Are you clear in your mind about the level of service you want?*
- *Have you articulated that to the individual involved?*
- *Do you feel the need to 'tread carefully' to ensure that the function gets carried out properly?*
- *Do you fret about the person's efficiency and wish the job was done better?*
- *Is there any awkwardness in your dealings?*
- *Does the service need support rather than giving support?*
- *Does it take up time and emotional energy?*

Consider these relationships long and hard, and resolve to keep your judgements about them pragmatically in the mental box marked 'functional'. Nobody is asking you to be brittle or bland in your dealings with these people in your life. They are likely to be very important for keeping things running smoothly, but you have not chosen them because of emotional engagement or needs; you have chosen them because they are the right people for the job you need to get done, and you and they should have a relationship that works efficiently.

WAYS TO IMPROVE YOUR PROFESSIONAL AND SUPPORT SERVICES BREAKEVEN

- *Be clear about what you want to see as the end result of a job well done.*
- *Make sure you have relayed this expectation to the person concerned.*
- *Consider the timing of any difficult conversation. When is the person in question most likely to be receptive?*
- *If you have small concerns, explain your overall satisfaction first.*
- *If you are dissatisfied with the level of service you are getting, have all your reasons ready in order to build your case.*
- *If you feel uncertain about your complaints and how you will express them, rehearse anticipated difficult conversations with a trusted friend.*
- *Communicate effectively, maintaining eye contact and listening actively to any relevant points the person concerned has to make about the job in hand.*
- *If you are on the phone, smile. It makes you sound a*

Second Stage

nicer, calmer person.

- *If you think someone else could do the job better and cause you less angst, change the personnel and reduce the time you need to put into that area of your life.*
- *You have categorised these people as 'professionals', so treat them as such by having high expectations of the role they play and the service they provide in your life.*
- *Build into the time you expend on making sure they do the job properly an ongoing assessment of the way they play their part in the smooth running of your life.*
- *Show your appreciation for a job well done. Remember to say thank you.*

Home Breakeven

Your Stocktake should have concentrated your mind on your home, what it means to you and how much time you are prepared to invest in keeping it as a comfortable and stress-free environment. You have reached a Breakeven figure of what time you need to look after the things you currently possess. This section is going to help you reduce that figure, while maintaining the necessary level of order and comfort. It may be useful to have a separate ring binder for the various checklists you can fill in – these will serve as a quick reference in the future.

Your inventory of your fixtures and fittings should have identified which things you use and need, and the rest you will have either thrown away or placed in a holding area until you are quite sure you can bear to be parted from them. When you were carrying out the Stocktake you eliminated these items because they were neither useful nor beautiful. Because the Audit is not about being prescriptive and you are the one setting the rules, take some time now to go back and double-check your decision to throw them away.

Ask yourself these questions:

- *It may not be useful or beautiful, but does it have sentimental value?*
- *If you bought it yourself, why did you buy it?*
- *What have you used it for in the past?*
- *If the function it performed arose again, what would you use?*
- *Have you used it in the last six months?*
- *If you keep it, where will it live? Is it worthy of going on display or is there an appropriate cupboard?*
- *Is it part of something you've planned to do, e.g. a hobby kit? If so, do you still want to do it and should it be transferred to your wish list?*

Are you still fearful of consigning any of your belongings to the scrapheap even if you've confirmed they don't have a place in your life? If so, you could do what I did during my first Audit. I thought I was so irrevocably attached to some belongings, mainly clothes, paperwork and books, that, lacking an adequate holding area, I rented temporary storage. These small units, usually on trading estates on the outskirts of town, are relatively cheap and I congratulated myself on finding a quick-fix solution to my surplus stuff that freed up immediate time but avoided throwing anything out. It certainly did both those things – but in the year my stuff sat in that storage container I actually only needed one thing from it – a pair of gloves! Just think how many new pairs of gloves I could have bought with the money I spent proving I really didn't need any of those things. So while I don't want to be responsible for you regretting having thrown something out, do make sure you are going to appreciate or use it if you keep it.

WAYS TO IMPROVE YOUR HOME CONTENTS BREAKEVEN

- *Focus on one room at a time.*
- *Chuck anything that's on permanent display that reminds you of a sad or unhappy time, an unkind person or a failed love affair. Negative waves can just as easily be emitted by objects as by people.*
- *A place for everything and everything in its place. Having made a conscious decision to keep a household item, ornament or piece of furniture, allocate it the appropriate space.*
- *Make sure you only have current catalogues or brochures or TV listings magazines.*
- *Throw out duplicate items.*
- *If a room still feels overcrowded, re-audit the contents to make sure there is nothing else you can dispense with.*
- *Clear surfaces. They should not be dumping areas where clutter can build up. Either choose to have items on display and put them in specific places, or store them in a drawer or cupboard.*

If you have ended up with a quantity of things you plan to get rid of you may want to consider making some profit by selling them (see Money Breakeven on page 151), or recycling them or donating them to a charity shop (see Citizenship Breakeven on page 164).

Cupboards, drawers and shelves

The contents of your wardrobe and the drawer where you keep the beauty and grooming products you use will be covered in the Image section. But what about all the other cupboards and storage areas in your home? Some will contain useful and relevant things, but others will hide belongings you have stored away out of sight and out of mind. Now is the time to sort through them and clear the decks of anything surplus to your life's requirements. Following similar principles to those you employed with your clothes, match the hidden-away stuff with the use you make of it.

My own cupboards and storage areas were:

- *in the kitchen for food and cooking utensils*
- *in the dining room for crockery, glasses and silver*
- *in the utility room for cleaning and laundry products*
- *in the sitting room for books, family games, DVDs and CDs*
- *in the office for paperwork, files, reference material and stationery*
- *in the bedroom and airing cupboard for linen and towels*
- *in the shed for tools, decorating hardware and gardening implements*
- *in the garage for cars, bicycles and related items*

Be ruthless and make contents inventories for each holding space. For example, when I tackled my kitchen cupboards I pulled out all the odd tins and packets of food that didn't have a place in my regular cooking and entertaining repertoire and either used them up or threw them away. It was shocking how many had passed their 'best before' date. I then made a definitive checklist of the dry and tinned goods I felt I needed to have in stock and the kitchenware that I needed and would use regularly. Being a constant and daily cook, I had accumulated hordes of utensils and had many duplicates. Would I ever need eight roasting trays? I think not! They were whittled down to four of different sizes. The same applied to everything in the kitchen.

The key to achieving cupboard clarity is to make headings for the contents of each area and then list under them the individual items you are storing there. Pedantic and boring, I know – but worth it in the end. The same de-cluttering principles you used when dealing with individual rooms apply, although as you'll probably be dealing with smaller items that may not be in regular use, it may take a little longer and need a few extra criteria.

Ask yourself these questions:

- *Is it in full working order?*
- *If not, is it repairable? (Remember that even if the answer is 'yes', a new one may be cheaper.)*
- *Is the item time-sensitive, e.g. out-of-date paperwork, dry goods past their 'best before' date?*
- *If it's a nostalgic keepsake, should you start a Memory Box to hold precious archive material?*
- *If it belongs to someone else in your home, are they sure they need it?*
- *Are you keeping it because it 'might come in useful'?*

The more ordered your stowed-away items are, the less time they will take up in your life: you won't waste time looking for them. The lack of muddle below the surface will reinforce the focus you want in the rest of your life, making Breakeven easier to achieve across the board.

WAYS TO IMPROVE STORAGE CONTENTS BREAKEVEN

- *Make sure you aren't making excuses to hang on to things 'just in case' – ask yourself honestly when the last such eventuality happened.*
- *If it's a shame to hide an item in a cupboard, consider where it would look good out on display.*
- *Treat your fridge as one of your storage areas and use it efficiently. In general, the more you have in it, the better it will work.*
- *If you are short of storage space consider other possibilities such as the cavities under bench seating, wall-hung containers and pocket organisers on the backs of doors.*
- *Install shelves inside fitted cupboards to help order behind closed doors. If you know you won't put things away as you use them, introduce a pending basket for a once-a-week tidying session. Then use it!*

Plan to sort out your cupboards over a period of time. It's likely that there will be quite a lot of surplus things in them because in the past you will have pushed them out of sight because you didn't have the time or inclination to consider whether you really needed them or not. From now on, every time you buy something really think about the place it's going to have in your room, and make sure

Second Stage

it's going to be useful or beautiful or so important to you personally that you just can't live without it.

FILLING IN YOUR STORAGE INVENTORY

- *See chart 29.*
- *Give each cupboard, drawer, shelf or other storage space a name or short description to identify it.*
- *Define the general category of things it is going to contain.*
- *Write down the contents, using sub-headings if appropriate.*
- *Make a note of the condition of everything in the cupboard.*
- *This will enable you to create tick lists of things you would like to renew/update or replace.*

Chores: shopping

Was one of the cupboards you did a blitz on your kitchen store cupboard? We're about to move on to chores, and for many people the weekly shop is one of the most time-consuming chores of all. The Inventory of your food store cupboard is also the foundation for your Shopping List. You need to keep stocked up on basic dry and non-perishable goods, with a 'just-in-time' discipline so that all you have to get each week are the fresh provisions. And don't forget supermarket items that aren't food: items that belong in the wine rack, in the bathroom cabinet or under the sink. The Shopping List, chart 30, has all the headings you should need to make sure the weekly big shop is not a long shop.

The Life Audit

FILLING IN YOUR SHOPPING LIST

- *Enter the fresh produce you buy regularly every week so it forms part of a template. Tick items as you need them.*
- *Also enter any of the dry goods or staples that you use regularly in quantity, so that they are never forgotten.*
- *Number the headings in the order you usually go around the supermarket.*
- *If someone else ever does the shopping for you, put down the brands you prefer.*
- *Adopt a 'just-in-time' philosophy by making sure you check and replenish your staples on a regular basis.*
- *Don't be a fresh food snob – quick-cook frozen vegetables such as peas can be just as good for you as fresh, as can some tinned fruit in juice.*
- *Eggs are the definitive fast food. Make sure you always have them in stock.*
- *Remember the needs of any non-human members of your household, e.g. petfood, cat litter.*
- *Keep the list in a specific place in the kitchen, such as pinned to the inside of the store cupboard or kept in place by a fridge magnet, so that you can add to it as you think of things you need.*
- *Come up with a series of meals that would see you through a week or weekend when you can't get to the shops and that use ingredients you would normally have in stock or in the freezer. You can use the Meal Planner, chart 28, to do this.*
- *If you can order your shopping online, do it! Make a*

Chores: housework

When I was writing my lists of chores I found it tempting to set unrealistic goals for housework and then had to put a lot of energy into making sure I fulfilled them. As a result I had to establish rigid routines to stop me making a meal out of the things that needed to be done. I was very aware that this area of my life needed to be carefully ordered to prevent it becoming a mountain I would struggle to climb every day.

If you share your home with a partner, family or friends, upkeep and cleaning may well be something you think needs to be a shared responsibility. You may decide to talk to the others about the list of jobs you've come up with and see if they want to alter anything. That should lead on to a discussion about the division of labour. The problem you will have with this approach – unless everyone is exceptionally equable, or you have the power to coerce – is that you are carrying out this Audit for yourself, and therefore the Breakeven position you are seeking is yours and yours alone. So the realistic Breakeven you finally settle on has to be achievable by you, and not dependent on the good offices of others unless they are guaranteed.

Geoff, 67, says that if household duties are shared it's important to be mindful of the division of labour in relation to who has the most time. 'At first when I retired I didn't do much around the house. Then it became obvious that I should get more involved, because Sue was still working. To be honest, I was finding my days a bit empty anyway. I don't know why I didn't help more immediately – I think we were both stuck in the rut of it being Sue's domain. We had a few problems at first because I really wasn't very good, and certainly not up to her standards. I did discover a new hobby in cooking, though, and I actually enjoy my daily forays to the local shops.' 'I had to bite my tongue quite a lot in the beginning,' admitted Sue. 'But that's where the Life Audit came in useful, because it was a non-judgemental way of writing down what needed to be done and Geoff could see for himself without me nagging or getting wound up about it. He got more thorough the more he did it, and he really came into his own with the food shopping which also led to him cooking the evening meal.'

Kate, 30, decided to turn her housework routine on its head when she came up with her bespoke plan for her one-bedroom flat. 'I decided not to do any daily chores at all apart from making the bed, and just have an hour-long blitz every Saturday morning. What doesn't get done, doesn't get done. Then once a month I invite friends around for supper, or my parents come over for Sunday lunch, and I really go to town on the cleaning. I hate it so much, that's the only thing that will make me do it.'

Your Stocktake should contain a realistic interpretation of the daily, weekly, monthly, quarterly and annual household jobs you wish to see done. You should also know what cleaning materials and products you need. Just like Kate, Geoff and Sue, you now need to write your own personal housework routine. Your Housework Breakeven will be very much a bespoke plan for you and designed by you, but having seen what you have achieved over your auditing time you are now in an informed position to make it more efficient.

Ask yourself these questions:

- *Are you happy with the amount of time you have committed to domestic chores?*
- *Would you add other chores to your routines if you had time?*
- *Does the amount of housework you achieve satisfy what needs to be done daily, weekly etc.?*
- *Are you quite sure you are being realistic?*
- *Are there any pockets of chores you are making too much of?*

Now use the Housework Planner to draw up the definitive 'to do' list that you intend to stick to. You will need to make enough copies to cover every room. Don't skip the detail. The more pedantic you are, the easier it will be for other people to help you.

FILLING IN YOUR HOUSEWORK PLANNER

- *See chart 31.*
- *Write down the name of each room.*
- *For each room write down the chores listed in your Stocktake.*
- *Write them down in the order they should be done.*
- *Don't forget to include your gardening requirements if they are only basic and/or you only have a small outside space. If not, you might want*

to adapt the Home Maintenance Checklist, chart 33, to make a Garden Maintenance Checklist and enter in the appropriate places items such as spring and autumn pruning, spring seed sowing, autumn maintenance of paths and fences, fortnightly grass-mowing in the growing season and so on. But remember that, if you regard your garden as a source of pleasure rather than a maintenance chore, it (or part of the activity) should come under Leisure (see chart 21).

Perhaps you can improve your Housework Breakeven by taking a look at the following list of time-saving tips supplied by other Life Auditors. Room by room, see if any of the following work for you, build them into your routine and trim the time needed to achieve your personal Breakeven position accordingly.

WAYS TO IMPROVE YOUR HOUSEWORK BREAKEVEN

Kitchen

- *To speed up the nasty job of oven cleaning put a bowl of water in the oven while it is still hot after cooking.*
- *Always line your grill pan with foil so you never need to scour off burnt-on food.*
- *A tiny drop of baby oil or cooking oil rubbed into stainless-steel surfaces with a soft clean cotton cloth will prevent fingerprints and other smears from marking the shine.*

- Oven cleaning spray cleans oven glassware if sprayed on and left for half an hour.
- Mild window cleaning sprays and creams give a great shine to chrome finishes on toasters, kettles and taps.
- Put spare bin liners inside your waste bin so that as one fills and is removed there is another ready to take its place.
- A bowl of hot water in a freezer speeds up the thawing process when there are blocks of built-up ice.
- A dessertspoon of washing powder brought to a simmer with some water in a pan containing burnt-on food will clean it in minutes.

Sitting room

- If you have pets, try this for upholstery cleaning: wear rubber gloves, hold your hands under a running tap, shake off excess water and then plump up cushions and smooth down sofa covers and throws. The gloves will pick up all the hairs, which can then be rinsed off. (It works well for clothes, too.)
- A hacksaw blade dragged over a carpet removes pet hairs brilliantly, at the same time bringing up flattened pile. Do it before you vacuum.
- Don't waste money, time or storage space on spray polishes. A soft cloth will get rid of dust on wood furniture, supplemented by occasional gentle damp wiping over. Use a mist sprayer, available from garden centres, and spray the duster not the furniture.
- If you have an open wood-burning fire only clear the ash once a week – let a good base build up.

- Use anti-static dusting cloths, especially on electrical appliances such as televisions and sound systems.

Bathroom

- Make cleaning the bath and shower compulsory for everyone after use.
- Use non-rinse cleaners.
- Encourage other users to add a capful of bubble bath when running their bath, which makes cleaning easier afterwards.
- Don't scrub at limescale on taps or showerheads. Soak pads of kitchen roll in white vinegar and wrap around item, cover with a plastic bag secured with an elastic band and leave overnight. Simply rinse clean the next morning.
- If you have a condensation-prone bathroom that attracts mildew and causes glass and chrome to smear, invest in a couple of semi-tropical plants to absorb some of the humidity and use a demister spray on your mirrors and taps.
- At the beginning of cleaning the bathroom, squeeze some hair-removing cream into plugholes. By the time you get round to rinsing basin, bath or shower that yucky job will be non-existent!

Laundry

- If you can afford it, never hand wash sweaters – take them to the dry cleaners. Washed woollies require time, space and special washing products and are spectacularly easy to ruin. Alternatively, only buy

Second Stage

machine washable sweaters.

- Try tumble drying clothes and putting them immediately on hangers to see if you can get away with not ironing them.
- My ironing philosophy involves two sorts of clothes: those that get hung up when wet and drip dry ready to wear, and those that need to be ironed just before wearing because even the smallest wardrobe crush creases them.
- If you're like me you'll appreciate having your ironing board up and ready all the time, maybe in a guest room. Alternatively, install a pull-out, ever-ready ironing board.
- Don't let the ironing pile stack up unless you are someone who makes time to plough through the chore. Put the stuff on hangers and iron to order – then you won't forget you've got them. Many male Life Auditors had ironing that day's shirt as part of their morning routine.
- If you spend ages sorting socks into pairs, only buy one colour or else buy madly distinctive ones. Invest in a mesh wash bag and count them into the machine and out again after each wash.
- Always iron before items become bone-dry, i.e. when they are iron-'damp' (or spray with a mister) and then let clothes and linen have a good airing.

Bedroom

- Achieve high-speed duvet cover changing by turning the cover inside out when you strip the bed before washing and drying it. Then dive into it, grasp the top two corners from the inside as well as the top two corners of the duvet itself, and shrug the cover over the top right side out.

- Colour code your sheets and duvet covers with marker pen on tape labels to identify easily whether they are single, double or kingsize.

- Making the bed instantly makes a room seem tidy even if you haven't touched anything else yet.

- Clothes lying around always make a room look untidy. Either put worn clothes in a laundry basket or hang them up for further wear. Don't use a bedroom chair or the floor as a dumping ground.

General time-saving principles

- Always clean from the top down – cobwebs first, carpets last.

- Always dust, change sheets and plump cushions before vacuuming.

- Multi-tasking is the way to save time with housework. Do the ironing or sew on buttons while watching TV.

- Same principle: combine quiet repetitive chores, such as wiping over kitchen surfaces, with a duty phone call or one of those tedious calls via a call centre where you know you are likely to wait ages to be connected to the right department or a human being.

- Clean the outside of windows vertically and the inside horizontally so you can quickly tell which side any difficult smears are on.

- Add even more value by exercising while cleaning.

Second Stage

> *Dance with the vacuum, stretch with the duster, jog on the spot while ironing, do stomach curls and buttock clenches while washing up.*
>
> - *Get into the habit of never leaving a room empty-handed. There's always something that should be elsewhere. Pick it up and get it on its way.*
> - *Line all drawers and cupboards with domestic lining paper. This will save you time when you clear and clean them out and will simply need periodic replacing.*
> - *Rubber gloves are easier and quicker to take off if you sprinkle some talcum powder inside.*

A note here about partners, children and fellow residents if you are flat- or house-sharing: get them to understand that housework is not one person's responsibility if you have all got equally busy and committed lives, and that it's fair that everyone should do their bit. With children, if they're biddable and you have the time and patience, train them as soon as you can to air their own beds and rooms, to sort and even do their own washing and ironing, and to leave the bathroom and sitting room neat and tidy after they've used them. Good luck!

Several families of Life Auditors offered different ways to achieve this from establishing star charts to agreeing a family rota for chores. 'It all seemed like hard work in the beginning when I decided to make my three kids help out in the mornings,' 36-year-old Donna said. 'Getting them to do simple things like clearing away after breakfast and tidying their rooms before leaving for school needed so much organising and nagging it would have been quicker to do it myself. But after a couple of weeks it all suddenly started happening like clockwork. Now they each get up and organise their own breakfasts, clear away afterwards, make their beds and get their school stuff ready while I'm doing the packed lunches and dealing with the dog. It's brilliant.'

Getting through the pain barrier of introducing a new routine does seem to be a common experience, with perseverance paying off. The Davies family, who have four children between the ages of six and fifteen, have divided the house into six 'areas' on a family rota and change responsibilities weekly. 'That way you only have to be on bathroom and loo cleaning duty once every six weeks!' says the eldest, Euan. 'We're each in charge of our own rooms, and also have to make sure through the week that our "area" is kept clean and tidy.'

You must work out the system that suits you best, and there's a separate Housework Rota Chart (chart 32) on which to insert helpers' names or initials if you are able to share any of the chores. Finally, if you have managed to cut down on the time your domestic arrangements take, adjust your Breakeven accordingly.

There are three additional charts to enable you to keep tabs on household maintenance and decoration. As many of the checks and inspections are seasonal, the Home Maintenance Checklist (chart 33) is divided up accordingly. The Decorating Chart (chart 34) is for you to fill in as a useful reference list for your home, so you never have to measure up for wallpaper or guess a paint colour again. But do remember that, if doing up your home is something you look forward to, you need to consider carefully whether any element of it should go under Leisure.

Finally, (chart 35) there is a Household Information sheet. Enter on this the details of people you might need to contact in connection with the organisation of your family, home and possessions.

Image Breakeven

You may find people commenting that you seem different since you started doing the Life Audit. That's probably more to do with your attitude than with your appearance, since the Stocktake of your image should really have been no more than a situation report. At this stage of the Audit you should embark on a comprehensive Stocktake of the *active* clothes in your wardrobe, together with the nature of your personal grooming routines and the products and processes involved. You should be able to apportion the exact amount of time needed to achieve an acceptable Grooming Breakeven, and you should also have identified the basic items in your wardrobe that meet most of your life's public and private demands. You will also have started to define your particular style, with a collection of magazine cuttings and jottings of looks you have seen that you either like or definitely reject. So now, how to make sure that your Image Breakeven is as effective and efficient as it can be without forfeiting any individuality and flair?

Grooming

First, consider the grooming of your body beautiful. Take out your definitive list of products and processes. It should be easy to match what you do and what you use. That, then, is your grooming toolkit and your face and body maintenance plan. Have you addressed all these areas: hair, face, eyebrows, shaving, other unwanted hair, skin, elbows, hands, nails, feet, body odour, fragrances?

Ask yourself these questions:

- *Do your grooming routine, hairstyle and make-up reflect your age and fashion trends?*
- *How much thought do you put into the products you buy? Do you grab the cheapest, the one that features in the trendiest advert, the one you've always used?*
- *Are you sure the product you end up with is the right one for you?*
- *Does it do its job properly?*
- *Might there be a better product on the market?*

You need to make sure you have got the best products and appliances for your needs and budget. If not, research the market until you find the right ones. As you purchase them, consider each and every bottle, tube or pot of soap, shaving foam, face cream, powder, hair dye colour, aftershave, fragrance and so on, and make its inclusion a purposeful choice. Now, make up your mind to stick with that brand and don't be tempted to double up with another product that will do the same job and that just happens to catch your eye even though you still have plenty of your original choice left. Of course you can experiment with other brands if you want to, but not until you have to buy a fresh supply.

Individual grooming routines are part of the preparations each of us makes to achieve a state of readiness for the day ahead. This process of rewriting your Grooming Breakeven is therefore difficult to generalise about because of its intensely personal quality. I know people who can spend an hour or more enjoying their daily ablutions, whereas my personal daily routine takes 15 minutes. You may not want to feel compelled to save

Second Stage

time in this area other than by settling on what you use so as not to waste time and space with unwanted products. However, if you do want to crank extra time and value out of your grooming routines and product choices here are a few tips other Life Auditors have suggested.

WAYS TO IMPROVE YOUR GROOMING BREAKEVEN

- *Use a multi-purpose shower and shampoo gel.*
- *Keep your grooming staples in see-through zip bags so you can see things at a glance.*
- *Buy two of everything and put the second set in a similar series of see-through bags in your gym kit. That way there is never any risk of running out.*
- *Make appointments with hairdressers, barbers and beauticians for early in the day, before they fall behind schedule.*
- *Book your next appointment as you leave each time.*
- *Even if you prefer to wet shave, have an electric shaver ready charged to deal with five o'clock shadow or for mornings when you are pressed for time.*
- *Decant a little of every potion, liquid and cream into small travel pots. Not only will you then be ready to travel at a moment's notice, but if you run out you'll also have short-term reserve supplies until you next get to the shops.*
- *If your hair needs time-consuming blow-drying, invest in some Velcro rollers that take nano-seconds to put in after you have rough-dried your hair and achieve much the same effect in the time it takes to put your make-up on.*

- *Remember the adage about less being more? As you grow older it applies to make-up, which means less time in front of the mirror.*
- *Exchange notes with friends about products they recommend.*
- *Ask make-up counter assistants for advice, samples or demonstrations.*

If you have decided you can condense any of your grooming routine, you will be able to make a time adjustment on the Breakeven. You should also have worked out the frequency of any external appointments, such as with your hairdresser, during the Stocktake. If you have more than one salon treatment, try to commit one morning or one day to getting everything done in one fell swoop.

Wardrobe

Your Stocktake should have given you a definitive list of clothes you wear for specific events and for day-to-day living. Did you remove the others to a separate holding space? Now is the time either to pack them right away to consider in the appropriate season or to consign them to friends, the jumble sale or the charity shop. Is there much more room now in your wardrobe? You now need to hone that selection of clothes further, and weed out any duplications or spot where an element of one outfit could have a multi-function when teamed with another.

Your Wardrobe Breakeven should be a selection of outfits that will see you through the events of most days and a range of social occasions, whether they are simply

Second Stage

185

drinks at your local pub or an evening at the opera. You can of course keep extra outfits if you like, to ring the changes, but be totally honest with yourself if those outfits never do get chosen and it's the old favourite that does the job every time.

You may have found yourself in the same position as I did after a few days – for me, it was a revelation. I was shocked when it became staggeringly apparent that, even though my wardrobe was bulging at the seams, I seemed to exist on just three outfits – different combinations of a black skirt, black trousers, black jacket, jeans, black T-shirt, black jumper and white shirt. Black boots, flat pumps and flipflops saw me through every eventuality at the beginning of the month when I was keeping my Day Journal and writing down what I did with my time and what I wore. The clothes were all wash, drip-dry and wear, so could be turned round overnight. Fantastic! It seemed I could easily achieve a very efficient Breakeven without making any further effort.

However, I wasn't happy with that – and you may not be either, if the same applies to you. I knew that my clothes choices each day were a cop-out. While I had managed to eliminate time-wasting at the wardrobe door each morning, it wasn't because I had the perfect choice of clothes that truly reflected my lifestyle. In fact it was because I didn't! I was so overwhelmed by the different styles and types of outfits I had that I just went for old favourites time and time again.

Megan had a similar problem but for different reasons. 'I'd put on a bit of weight, and when I looked at my clothes choices each day I realised I was always choosing the baggy, comfort zone outfits which just reinforced how unhappy I was with my shape. So I threw them all out and *made* myself put on normal clothes – not tracksuits and big T-shirts.'

Publisher Rachel's statement acknowledged that, like me, she preferred wearing black clothes because they were slimming and could usually be relied upon to suit any occasion, so it lessened the room for error. 'The reason this is important to me is because I'm not confident about how well I carry off colourful clothes. I also could see that my wardrobe was pretty conventional and that I opted for classics and tailoring most of the time – again because they are hard to get wrong.'

I assumed that men had different wardrobe needs from women, but actually the principles are the same and, surprisingly, age doesn't seem to make much difference. Darren, 25, and 66-year-old Bill both provided me with virtually identical lists which, when shown to other chaps, seemed to be fairly representative. Both agreed they were lazy when it came to their clothes choices, Darren blaming lack of funds, Bill age/status conformity. Darren's combat trousers and trainers, apart from becoming dated, were increasingly unsuitable for some of the presentations he had to give as a junior account manager at an advertising agency. Bill, it seemed, was eternally trapped in dark chinos and pastel polo shirts.

There was nothing wrong with either of these men's appearances. In fact they both looked fine in their clothes. The issue was that they were wearing clothes that were a result of *not* thinking about their image. That would be all right if it was a conscious choice, but both men agreed they would like to be a little more distinctive and individual.

The critical eye you employ during the Audit will at least ensure you un-muddle your clothes, and with luck will also enable you to enjoy wearing them or making changes if you choose. The next stage is to test whether what you actually keep in your closet has anything in common with the style features you have been thinking about and collecting. Here's your chance, if you want, to break out from your safe looks and be more individual – to allow your clothes to reflect the real you.

You need to define more succinctly how it is you want to look, and to see if your current wardrobe contains any elements that match that ideal. If your conclusion is that it's too much of a mismatch, you might be prepared to settle for what you have while in the meantime compiling a wardrobe wish list that you can start to assemble when funds allow. You can do this by collating your likes and preferences from your Image Stocktake and testing each current outfit against it to see how it perfoms in the style stakes. You should then be able to start filling in your definitive clothes list, making a note of items you want to buy further along the line.

Ask yourself these questions:

- *Are you trapped in a one-type outfit rut?*
- *Do you have too many of one sort of thing?*
- *When did you last check your correct sizing?*
- *How often do you check your back view?*
- *Define the compelling element of your favourite clothes, e.g. comfort, formality, neatness, co-ordination.*

Achieving your definitive long-term look and style effectively should be an ongoing project, with fashion, age and seasonality as continuously shifting influences. But you don't need to devote lots of time or money to keep a happy balance and reach an easy Breakeven level.

WAYS TO IMPROVE YOUR WARDROBE BREAKEVEN

- Have a relationship with each garment you own. Really love it and cherish it.
- Buying the best quality you can and looking after it will help.
- Hang and store clothes in sensible order, by colour or type.
- Having hangers you love, padded or wooden, will encourage you to use them.
- Don't cram your clothes into a small space – you'll waste time looking for them. A coat needs about 12cm on the rail, shirts, trousers and skirts about 5cm each, a suit about 8cm.
- Have three needles ready threaded with black, white and clear thread for urgent repairs.
- Mentally note when people compliment you on a particular outfit and analyse what it is about the ensemble that has worked – is it the cut, the colour, the combination?
- Know your good points and choose styles that accentuate them. Skim over your bad points.
- If your wardrobe needs lots of improving, don't complicate your clothes: simple is good.
- If money is tight or your taste is suspect, keep your basic wardrobe in neutrals such as black, cream, navy and taupe and make your fashion statements by adding scarves, sweaters, bags etc. in the colours, textures and shapes of the moment.
- You did it for your Stocktake, so continue to be aware of

other people's looks and styles around you, on the train, in magazines, on television.

- *Continue to have a conscious view on what you do and don't like and ponder how you can include in your existing wardrobe ideas that appeal.*
- *Look upon a little window shopping as time well spent. Visit a favourite high street or department store and see what shapes and colours seem to be in fashion.*
- *Use mail order and the Internet! There are so many great catalogues for browsing and shopping without leaving the comfort of your own home.*
- *When planning an actual purchase, be very focused on the item you want and don't be deflected.*
- *If it's something new to accompany an existing outfit, wear that outfit to go shopping.*
- *When trying on new clothes, wear the shoes you intend to wear with those clothes.*
- *If fashion is a hobby for you, make sure you build in time to enjoy planning, thinking about and shopping for your wardrobe.*
- *Reappraise your style and carry out a clothes Stocktake twice a year.*
- *Have one 'safe' outfit that will do for all sorts of occasions.*

Now fill in your Wardrobe Inventory. Make use of the template supplied here, but remember it is not prescriptive and there is space for you to customise.

Money Breakeven

Is money making your world go around, or has conducting the Audit of your finances just left your head spinning? In many cases, it was frustration with money matters that prompted people to undertake the Life Audit.

Auditing your money required you to come up with some pretty straightforward information, and of all areas it should have been the most difficult to misinterpret because the earning and spending of money are cold, hard facts. If you filled in the charts properly you should have supplied the unforgiving data that cannot be fudged or massaged. If you did cheat, particularly with your spending habits, you were only fooling yourself. Go back and get real!

Your Income and Expenditure chart should have pointed up any imbalance. The Breakeven position you need to hit should be crystal-clear. If you are in deficit, it's

Second Stage

191

simply the difference between the two. If you are actually in a positive equity situation, give yourself a pat on the back. Finding your Money Breakeven is about making the most of current opportunities to earn money, making the money you spend go further, and turning the management of your money into an organised, accurate and not time-intensive task. Even if you are in the black do read the following Life Auditors' advice to see if you can spot anything that could improve your lucky lot further. It's a long and carefully thought out list of money-saving tactics and ways of maximising your earning potential without changing jobs, while minimising your time commitment to money management.

WAYS TO IMPROVE YOUR MONEY BREAKEVEN

Money organisation

- *Start a ring binder file (or files) now, with separate sections as appropriate, for all statements and financial paperwork.*
- *Empty your purse or wallet every day and put receipts on a stationery spike so that when you come to file them all you need to do is push a paper tie through the holes and put them in a monthly dated envelope. Then they'll be roughly in date order.*
- *Set aside the same time each week to balance the books.*
- *Paying bills 'just in time' enables you to keep your money in the bank longer – useful if it's an interest-earning current account.*
  The trade-off is that you have to diarise payment dates

scrupulously. If you don't feel up to this, pay bills as soon as they come in and then forget about them.

- Better still, wherever possible pay bills by direct debit, which makes it easier to budget and saves you time.

Banking, investments and money management

- Submit your bank manager to the same scrutiny you applied to your doctor.
- Internet banking can save you loads of time if you can process your transactions quickly. Relay any complaints to your bank and give them a chance to rectify the problem before giving up.
- Look into opening a high-interest deposit account, and the moment you get paid put as much as you can into it, transferring back into your current account what you need to make payments.
- Take the offer of an overdraft facility even if you don't need it. Should you ever go into the red, accidentally or not, it will prevent you being charged for an unauthorised facility.
- Shop around for the best deals on credit cards, borrowing and saving, and review regularly.
- Don't waste time thinking about investments until you have cleared all your debts.
- Spread your investment risk.
- Mystery shop your mortgage lender – present them with your case as though you were with another lender, and see what sort of mortgage repayment model they come up with.

Second Stage

193

- *Alternatively you could menace your mortgage lender – same principle, only this time just be yourself and say you are looking around for the best offer and thinking of moving.*
- *Make sure you are getting all your tax concessions and benefits.*

Comparison shopping

- *Type 'cheap . . .' followed by the item into an Internet search engine. The resulting list of sites will give you a feel for the cheapest prices both on and off the high street.*
- *Check out specialist magazines for comparison price lists and product reviews.*
- *Most major cities have areas that specialise in particular goods, such as London's Tottenham Court Road for electrical goods and Hatton Garden for jewellery. Prices are often keenly competitive.*

Home

- *Shop around for the best deal on utilities such as electricity and gas.*
- *Anticipate household repairs, renewals and general maintenance you will need to organise. The time gained will allow you to get competitive quotes and look out for special offers.*
- *When getting quotes from builders and decorators ask them if they can access trade-only wholesale suppliers for ready-made kitchen, units, bedroom furniture and bathroom suites.*
- *If there's something useful rather than beautiful on your*

wish list, keep an eye out in the For Sale columns in your local newspaper for secondhand goods in mint condition.

- Factory shops exist at most large manufacturers, and often goods with the tiniest blemishes can be picked up at rock-bottom prices.
- Visit your nearest architectural salvage yard, get friendly with the owner and tell him if you are trying to source something in particular.
- Keep up-to-date on local property values by looking in your local paper. Talk to estate agents about what adds value to a property such as yours.

Communications, IT and electrical goods

- To make sure you get the most suitable and cost-effective tariff, keep a diary of your line usage before choosing a mobile phone or line provider.
- Students and parents of students can often get special discounts on computers and software.
- Don't be a snob about supermarket electrical goods and gadgets. They are often good-value basic models, and the features they lack may well be ones you wouldn't use anyway.

Clothes

- Consider having a clothes-swapping party with same-size friends.
- Unless you are making investments in key pieces, don't buy designer high fashion. Look in supermarkets or on the high street for copycat versions of catwalk creations.

Second Stage

- But if you are buying a classic, timeless key item for your wardrobe buy the best – it will last.
- Learn to make your own clothes or source a local tailor/dressmaker and get them to copy designs.

Cars

- Compare the trade-in price with the suggested book value you could ask for your old car if you sold it privately. There is often a significant difference.
- Suggest to the dealer you may pay by cash for your new car, and see what the price falls to.
- Car supermarkets offer bargain prices.
- As does importing your new car, which can save you more than quarter the UK book price, although you are advised to use one of the import agencies advertised in car magazines, who understand the pitfalls.

Seasonal buying and selling

- There are times of year when some retailers are keen to shift stock as trade is slow. For instance, in a mild winter the January sales are full of coats and boots, and saletime in a cold, wet summer is great for seasonal clothes and swimwear.
- Christmas is a good time to buy a car.
- Summer is best for jewellery shopping.
- Spring is best for selling a house.

Holidays and travel

- Is the location of your home suitable for holiday house-swapping?

- Check out the Apex fares on public transport such as trains, available if you book in advance. Pre-planning, which should be part of your life now, can save you a lot.
- If your employer has a travel department, see if there are budget schemes or special corporate arrangements you can take advantage of.
- Do some research and use local bus services to get to and from stations and airports.

Insurance

- Make sure you aren't under-insured, or your insurer will discount any claim you make. Go back over your Home Stocktake and put a replacement value against the contents of each room. Take photos of important valuables or antiques, ask if they need to be separately itemised on the policy and/or require an extra premium, and keep your insurer informed.
- Make sure you know what you would get if items were damaged. Would it be new for old, or is yours an indemnity policy where a deduction is made for wear and tear?

Food

- Supermarkets start marking down food in the afternoon. Try shopping at 4p.m. rather than at 11a.m. Similar reductions are made at the end of the week and just before bank holidays. Pop surplus supplies in your freezer.
- Likewise, visiting a local market towards the end of the day will enable you to buy reduced produce, although the variety may also be less.

Second Stage

- Look into buying food and booze direct from the supplier. Farms and wine importers will often sell direct and deliver to your door, saving time and money.
- Buy in bulk if you can, and see if you can shop at your local cash and carry store.
- Make ingredients work for multi-meals, e.g. every time you buy a chicken or a joint of meat plan to stretch it out. Make extra gravy to add to leftovers, bulk up with vegetables and top the mixture with potato to make a pie. Boil up the carcass or bones, experiment with herbs and seasoning, and add noodles or pasta shapes to make a broth.
- Make 'waste not want not' your mantra, and become fanatical about not throwing any food away.
- Don't buy ready-washed salads and vegetables. They take seconds to do yourself. The time saved is negligible and the difference in cost colossal.
- The same applies to ready-packed vegetables. Instead buy them loose and pick out exactly the number you need.
- Plan meals and stick to a shopping list.

Entertainment and eating out

- If you are longing to try a special restaurant but daunted by the cost, see whether they do set-price lunches or bar menus which will enable you to savour the atmosphere, service and cuisine without breaking the bank.
- If you often go to the cinema or theatre, enquire about season tickets.

- Look out for special dining-out vouchers in the national press.

Miscellaneous shopping tips

- The police and transport lost property offices have regular bargain-filled sales of unclaimed goods.
- Consider buying reconditioned anything. As long as it's from a reputable company, items really can be as good as new and a whole lot cheaper.
- Become a cheeky shopper and always ask for extras to be thrown in or discounts to be given.

And finally, why not make some money?

- There are lots of places where you can sell unwanted articles. Take a pitch at a car boot sale – big popular ones are the best, and remember to take lots of change and carrier bags. Internet auction sites can be useful – do plenty of research and monitor the sales progress of similar articles. For antiques and valuables you can go through a dealer – a specialist if appropriate. Alternatively try a saleroom – get free valuations and estimates from auctioneers, who can sometimes do this just from a photo.
- Is your home interesting, beautiful or just plain suitable enough to be a location for TV, films or advertising commercials? Contact location agencies (look them up in Yellow Pages) to find out.
- Could you earn a bit of cash by renting out any spare parking capacity you might have in your drive if you live near a station or an area of town where parking is restricted?

Second Stage

- *If you live near the location of some major annual event, have you considered letting your whole house out at the pertinent time?*
- *Can a spare bedroom earn money from bed and breakfast or a lodger?*
- *Could you make money from selling anything you make on a hobby basis?*
- *Always check out the legal and taxation repercussions.*

Work Breakeven

Whether it's office work, study, full-time homemaking, even the business of full-time job-seeking, work forms an enormous part of life. Your Stocktake should have identified the time you spend working and the amount of enjoyment and fulfilment you gain from doing it. Without a lottery win, a trust fund or inherited wealth it's a 'must-do' to keep a roof over your head and food in your belly. You don't have to like it, but you do have to do it. We're not talking specifics here. We're talking about the hours you put into your daily graft, whatever that is.

If you're happy in your job

Let's assume first that you are an employee doing a job you enjoy and therefore not looking for a career change. You have done a simple addition sum and worked out how many hours you spend working. You are now going to see if there's any room for improvement – to see if you can crank more time out of your current day. There's an ethical problem in extracting more useful personal time from your actual working *hours*, but have you considered how flexible your working *day* might be? Are you allowed to start early, to work late or at weekends? Can you work through lunch and breaks, and if so can you leave earlier? An early or late start might save time by enabling you to avoid the rush-hour traffic. Could you be paid on a performance-related basis, so you had the opportunity of working smarter and faster? Any freeing up of time can mean a tighter Breakeven. Can any of those periods of time, however short, be transferred to other areas of your life such as exercise or domestic chores or relationships?

If career advancement in your current job is one of your aims, you will want to make the most of the time you spend at work to progress that plan. Time efficiency and working smart are big subjects with different disciplines applicable to different workplaces, levels of seniority and types of employer.

If you're not happy in your job

But what if, despite all your good will and best endeavours, there are still mismatches of minutes and hours in a working day that are nothing to do with you? If there's a major problem, whether it's too much time on your hands or maybe too little time, don't just turn up and *be* there for the duration of the working day. It's still your life you are living, even though someone else is paying for these hours.

I've been both an employee and an employer, I've worked for large and small companies and run my own businesses. Shockingly, people management and motivation are often very poor in both business and industry. All too many bosses would really rather you didn't come up with bright ideas that require them to

(a) consider changing a working practice they've instigated, (b) address why you have time on your hands or why their expectations of what is achievable are unrealistic, and (c) authorise, manage and explain to their superiors a new task or application, however good the idea.

If career issues were on your Really Personal Information list, or if you are expected to be in the workplace for longer than it takes to do the job well and you are given no encouragement to take on other duties, there may be some spare time you can use. In those circumstances you have no need to feel guilty about putting the spare time you have identified to more personal use. This applies to virtually every work scenario from office job to shop work, from sales to catering. The same principles of making the most of time in the workplace apply everywhere.

First make sure there really is nothing more that the boss expects you to do. Then, instead of chatting to your mates, taking another ciggie break or tilting your monitor so you can discreetly play Solitaire, think about what you can do with this dead time. Actually it's thinking time, planning time, maybe even research time for some of your wishes, especially if they concern work or career. A word of warning, though: do make yourself fully aware of the company's rules concerning Internet and phone use for private purposes. Although it's often tolerated, in practice it's something that could be used against you in any disciplinary action. But it's unlikely there will be a clause in your contract forbidding you to think or make notes in any 'downtime' you identify at work.

So now you've found some time, what might you need to address? Perhaps the main thing you identified in your

Stocktake of your work was that you want a radically different working pattern – perhaps job-sharing, or cutting down on your days in one post to take up training for a completely different job. Transfer those findings to your Really Personal Information.

Giving up a job, or even changing it, is a big step and needs to be thought about very seriously with due consideration of all the consequences. Research fully the positions or career you want to pursue, and carry out an investigation to discover all your options. The third stage of the Life Audit explains how to tackle such major life changes. But if you have some thumb-twiddling time at work there's nothing to prevent you starting research now. If you want to move on within your current industry you are well placed to look at the trade press, to talk to people in other similar companies and to exchange notes with colleagues about the scope for advancement. There are many more guidelines on moving an ambition forward in the Audit's third stage. Just make sure at this point that you have fully established not only how efficiently you can make use of your time at work, but also how you feel about your job and prospects for the future.

From the following tips supplied by previous Life Auditors, pick and choose those that are most relevant to your own work situation, whether you're an ambitious high-flier or someone who's been stuck in the same rut for far too long and just wants out.

WAYS TO IMPROVE YOUR WORK BREAKEVEN

- *Research the options for starting and finishing earlier or later.*
- *See if you can work straight through breaks and claim the time at the end of the day or let it accumulate towards extra days off.*
- *Can your work be performance-related (i.e. it's the end result that counts, not the hours you put in)?*
- *Don't forget that work time may be paid-for time but it is still your life.*
- *Be clear about your work-related ambitions, try to identify routes to achieve them, and think about how you might address obstacles.*
- *Quantify your worth to your boss, and make sure you are doing your job as well as expected for the reward you are getting.*
- *Understand the criteria behind the setting of targets, and hit them or know the reasons why. If you have failed, be honest and informed about why you have done so.*
- *Set up your own checks and controls on your performance, have personal expectations of your work commitment and measure yourself against them constantly.*
- *Be proactive in exploring promotion prospects on a regular basis, and if there are none on offer ask what you can do yourself to prepare for when there are. Think about acquiring extra skills, shadowing someone else or taking on extra responsibilities.*

- *Approach your career path as a project that needs research, planning and organisation.*
- *Look at the bigger picture of your industry and see how representative your pay, conditions and opportunities are.*
- *Put yourself forward for training courses, and be involved in company motivation and incentive campaigns.*
- *Be highly organised, punctual and 'neat' in your presentation of everything from your leave forms to ordering more paper clips.*
- *Don't ever procrastinate about a task, and always deliver on time.*
- *Be honest, loyal and, within the bounds of diplomacy, frank with both your superiors and junior members of staff about your and their expectations. They will come to trust you and see you as someone prepared to take responsibility and tackle work issues head on.*

The daily commute

Finally, let's look at the time you spend getting to and from work. Unlike other journeys in your week, these daily trips will have a rhythm and routine of their own that might mean you can plan to use the time productively. If you commute by train or bus you will probably already be reading or getting more sleep. But you could also use the time for learning or as ongoing Audit time to make entries and progress some of your plans. Alternatively you could use that time to give your brain a mental workout: set it a memory task each day. Travelling by car has its own advantages, even if you find yourself stuck in traffic jams. You can listen to audio books on tape or CD, you can loosen up your neck and head, practise abdominal or (for women) pelvic floor exercises, or listen to favourite music that makes you feel happy. Sing along with it each morning and evening to give your vocal cords a workout and lift your spirits.

Leisure Breakeven

How did you get on defining what you mean by 'leisure'? Was it hard to clarify how much time you spend just doing something you find restful and relaxing? On the Balance Sheet you should have written down what makes up your leisure time and how much of it you actually get.

One person's leisure may well be another person's idea of hard work, so it's virtually impossible for me or anyone else to tell you how to add value to the hours you spend at leisure. For starters, if you optimise the time use it may suddenly not feel so relaxing after all. So breathe easy and relax – you don't need to make sure your leisure time is working hard for you as long as you are getting it and enjoying every minute of it!

Ask yourself these questions:

- *Is the amount of leisure you calculated in your Stocktake as much as you actually need and want?*
- *If it's made up of different sorts of activities, or indeed non-activities, are the proportions right?*
- *Are you sacrificing leisure time on your own, such as reading or swimming, because you can't fit it in alongside that lunch with a girlfriend or knockabout five-a-side in the park? And do you really miss having it?*
- *Could you have planned your leisure time better?*

- *Is there anything you would have changed about the way you spent it?*

Is leisure an area of your life to which you want to give more time and attention? If so, by the time you have finished the Breakeven report you should be able to do just that. Leisure is important because it's your switch-off restorative time, complementing sleep. You must be sure that you have allowed it the right amount of time and priority in your life and on your Balance Sheet.

Since only you can quantify what will enhance the time you spend being leisurely, there is no way that I or any other Life Auditor could come up with suggestions on how to improve your Leisure Breakeven. This really is personal stuff. But it's important, so have fun coming up with ideas that work for you.

Citizenship Breakeven

As you charted your days during the time-logging you should have been making notes about the time and interest you gave to matters outside your own personal needs and wants. Have you defined what you currently mean by 'citizenship', and what you do in your life that qualifies? Have you perhaps decided that being a better citizen is one of the things you'd like to make more time for? Or, while being aware of a distinct shortfall in your citizenship efforts, are you at a loss as to what you can do, especially at a time when you are trying to sort your own self out?

Did asking yourself the question, however, at least raise your consciousness about anything? Perhaps you had a momentary pang of guilt when you chucked away all those reusable supermarket carrier bags, drove to the local shops when you could easily have walked, refused a *Big Issue*, didn't opt for fair-trade food, only read the features section of the newspaper. . . . Or did asking yourself the question highlight the fact that you didn't know where to start?

The first thing to do is to look at your daily life and spot the opportunities. Now that you have your life Balance Sheet in front of you, that should be an easy exercise. There's your home, the routines and habits you follow, the purchases you make, the food you eat, the transport you use, the relationships you have, and most important of all the opinions and attitudes you hold. All these things offer opportunities to focus on citizenship. If you are a bewildered wannabe good citizen, it's no good blindly buying into the good citizen advice on offer. You need to make sure that the actions you decide to take are ones you genuinely endorse and that the causes you support are ones you are glad to be associated with.

Being informed is very important, whether it's at local, national or international level. So if you decide to change any aspect of your life, check it out first to understand *why* you have decided to do so. Don't just do it willy-nilly to make yourself feel good – though you undoubtedly will! Gather the evidence. Read newspapers. Look at the people supporting issues and evaluate what they say. Don't be a passive spectator while watching the news on TV. Interrogate yourself about how you are reacting to a news item, whether it's national politics or the problem of dogs fouling pavements in your town. Even if you occasionally find yourself bored to tears, keep your interest alive by making this an ongoing process so you can discover the issues that really do engage you.

Now, let's look at your day-to-day life. While the concept of citizenship is not always something to which you have allocated dedicated time, acts of being a good, responsible citizen can be as much a habit in the rote and pattern of your life as smiling or scratching your nose.

As with leisure, it's almost impossible to make concrete suggestions for improving the bottom line of your Breakeven position *timewise*. However, here are a few ideas to get you started on the citizenship road so that you can address the opportunities offered in daily life and choose to support them or not. The majority of suggestions are to do with being an informed and considerate consumer. If you want to be even more active in this area, there are a few suggestions from other Life Auditors at the end of the list.

WAYS TO IMPROVE YOUR CITIZENSHIP BREAKEVEN

- *Do you sort your rubbish out and recycle paper, cardboard, plastic bottles, tins and glass?*
- *Look at your shopping basket and see if you have bought fair-trade goods which guarantee that the people who have produced them have been paid a fair wage.*
- *Do you buy organic local produce, which means not only that you will be avoiding pesticides but that you will be buying food that has had less distance to travel, thus keeping fuel use to a minimum?*
- *How eco-friendly is your car? Do you try to drive smoothly and avoid sharp braking? Is your exhaust as clean as it might be?*

Second Stage

209

- *Do you know how to get the best performance from your car to optimise fuel consumption?*
- *Do you avoid using the car for short journeys?*
- *Do you turn your kitchen waste into compost?*
- *Do you conserve water by taking showers rather than baths?*
- *Do you conserve electricity by using energy-efficient light bulbs?*
- *Do you switch everything off at the mains rather than using standby?*
- *Is your home insulated?*
- *Do you try to buy furniture that has been made from reclaimed wood?*
- *Do you take your own shopping basket to the supermarket instead of using throwaway carrier bags?*
- *Have you considered using eco-friendly disposable nappies, or even washable ones? (Not forgetting, in the latter option, that the trade-off is more washing, i.e. you use more water and more electricity, and put more phosphates from washing powder into the drains.)*
- *Do you try to avoid using anything made of PVC?*
- *When buying new electrical appliances, is energy efficiency top of your 'must-have' features?*
- *Have you got skills that you could use to help or support a need or a cause?*
- *View any community or good citizenship activities as providing you with additional 'wind-down' time, especially if it's hands-on and brain-off.*
- *Help with group citizenship activities organised by national organisations or companies, and meet new people that way too.*

Soul Breakeven

Did you manage to find your soul in the Stocktake? The Breakeven position with your soul is about reaching a complete understanding of what you feel and really are deep inside. When you've stripped everything else away, put this book to one side, forgotten all about stocktaking and breakevens and time and motion, your soul is what you are left with. By thinking just a little about it in this Audit you should have a better idea of the shape it's in. Its characteristics may still be pretty indefinable, but you should at least be able to say whether your inner man or woman is joyous or tragic, strong or frail, spiritually nourished or starved of contemplation and serenity.

Unless you enjoy poignancy you are likely to want your soul to be joyous and at one with the body and world it inhabits, and maybe the God you worship. Most Life Auditors were keen to talk about what their soul was and how they kept it nurtured. Many said that their spirituality was interwoven with their appreciation of the things in their life that brought them joy and contentment. Religious believers linked it to their faith and convictions, the non-believers to finding their place in a universe has so many unknowns and imponderables.

So, now that you have done your Stocktake and reached this point here are some ways in which you can keep this very special part of you nurtured.

WAYS TO IMPROVE YOUR SOUL BREAKEVEN

- *Don't underestimate the importance of looking after your soul.*
- *Look back over your blessings counted and make a note of at least ten things that bring you joy. Put the list in your wallet or handbag.*
- *Pray – even if you are not sure to whom or what. If you're not comfortable with the concept of prayer, try meditation.*
- *Talk to someone you love who has died. Ask them a question and see if you can feel what their response would be.*
- *Explore spirituality and open your mind by talking to others, visiting practitioners, attending services.*
- *You don't have to explore obscure spiritual movements if you don't want to. More familiar institutions such as the Church of England offer support and specific courses for spiritually bereft people.*
- *Consider giving your soul a holiday by going on a retreat.*
- *If you are curious, there are loads of spiritual therapies and practices to research.*
- *Try not to regret the past or fear the future. Focus on the moment you are living in right now.*
- *Make space for things you find uplifting, and be joyful about positive things in your life and the world.*
- *When you hear music you like on the radio make a note of its title, and then record a compilation.*
- *If you feel bleak, try to find an approach that speeds*

*your recovery. Life Auditors variously suggested putting
your head down and waiting for the storm to pass,
acting happy and determining to fool yourself and
others, going for a brisk walk early in the morning
and coming back to a hearty breakfast, battening down
the hatches and watching favourite TV programmes,
cooking favourite meals, going to bed early.*

- *Start a file of cuttings that make you smile or feel cheered.
  Collect newspaper stories, quotes, tickets from a fun day
  out – anything that makes you happy when you see it.*
- *Chronicle the happy things in your life that are nothing
  to do with possessions or money.*
- *If something in your life is making your soul die a little,
  open any daily newspaper and put your own sadness in
  perspective by looking at other people's tragedies.*
- *Look upon your hidden self as a very special part of you
  to explore. Take time to contemplate all those aspects of
  the inner you in the Stocktake.*
- *Accept that everyone has a dark side – even if it's only
  off-white. Know yours.*
- *Use times when you are alone to try listening to silence.
  You may be surprised at the thoughts you suddenly hear.*
- *Find time in your life just to be still.*
- *Let yourself 'be'.*

Mortality Breakeven

The Stocktake on your mortality had two aspects. First you
addressed your emotional state regarding the Big D, and
second you established how organised (or otherwise) your

affairs would be for those left behind. Basically you will now be putting in place a readiness for death that equates with the sense of realism you should now feel you possess about your life.

Twenty-four-year-old Trisha felt comforted by her mother's explicit instructions regarding her funeral arrangements when she died tragically young from cancer. 'In the last weeks of Mum's life she talked about who she wanted to be there, what hymns and readings she wanted, and even what food I was to serve afterwards at the house. Of course it was still very hard for us all – but somehow it made it less awful knowing that she had been prepared to think about her death and face it.'

Jim, 67, was just as prepared in the practical sense, but for a different reason. 'I'm sorry, I can't face up to the prospect of dying and really don't want to think about it. However, making all the arrangements and letting my son know where the will is and who to contact when I die means that I really can now forget about it and get on with living.'

By this stage in the Audit you should have worked out what your feelings are regarding death, and whether they are as coherent as they ever could be about this hugely challenging subject. Have you done that? And have you now, like Jim, resolutely decided not to spend any more time thinking about the inevitable? Or has the process heightened your fears? If so, you need to decide how you are going to deal with these fears.

Ask yourself these questions:

- *Do you need to spend more time thinking about your mortality?*
- *Can you pinpoint which aspect of death is the main*

driver in your anxiety, e.g. the process of dying, fear of the unknown, the end of your life before you've done all you want to do, your concern about those left behind?

- *Can you think about your fear rationally? The Audit is encouraging you to address your health and spirituality and to make every minute count. Do you think there is anything else you can do?*

If your answer to the last question is 'yes', you must be stern with yourself and determine not to waste more living minutes worrying about those when you won't be. You have given it your best shot, and that's that. Maybe you will find some comfort from channelling your concern into the administration of events immediately after your death.

The final chart in this Breakeven section enables you to consider all the issues that will face your next of kin and others after you die. They will want to follow your wishes and this chart will answer every question they might have, from the funeral arrangements to the administration of your estate. Filling this in, telling them it exists and then putting it somewhere safe should be a comfort and lead you towards closure. Now get on with living.

FILLING IN YOUR WISHES ON THE IN THE EVENT OF MY DEATH CHART

- *See chart 37.*
- *State whether you want to be buried or cremated.*
- *Make sure the names and contact details of the*

*executors and solicitors are written down and
up-to-date.*

- *Make a note of where your will and other key
  documents are kept.*
- *Be very clear about your wishes regarding organ
  donation. Use the space provided to list donor cards.*
- *You are planning this for the bereaved, so anticipate
  how individuals will support each other and be
  comforted or need support.*
- *Allocate responsibilities for such things as dealing with
  the funeral director, organising the readings, contacting
  friends and relations, and booking or catering for the
  funeral tea or wake.*
- *Choose music, poetry, favourite readings. Indicate if you
  want particular people to participate.*
- *Consider writing something special and personal to
  loved ones for them to read and be comforted by.*
- *If you can't think of anything inspired at the present
  time, such as the readings or hymns, say so and leave
  the choice to your family and friends. Alternatively
  commit yourself now to putting time aside to do some
  more research, thinking and planning.*
- *Indicate if you want your ashes scattered anywhere
  particular.*
- *Are there any special words you would like engraved on
  a headstone, or do you want your family to choose
  them? Be mindful of different diocesan rules regarding
  headstones.*

Your Best Breakeven Position – wrapping up the second stage

Having carried out the process of timesaving and elimination you will have improved your Breakeven position and be able to redraw the way you deal with the 'must-dos' in your daily life. You will have made some adjustments to the time commitments you originally attached to various life areas after the Stocktake, so you should now be able to recalculate that Balance Sheet and adjust accordingly that final figure: the number of hours you have left to do something with.

Having found your best Breakeven position, saved yet more time and eliminated the negative, destructive or pointless aspects of your life, you are now in a position to look to the future. You've got that magic chunk of time to play with – a sum of as yet uncommitted hours. In financial terms that would be your disposable income after you've met all your standing orders and other fixed outgoings. But what will you be doing with it?

THE life ⏱ audit

third
stage

Margins for Growth – spot your potential

R ight at the start of the Audit you made some lists of wishes and regrets in your Really Personal Information. Having now looked in close detail at all the aspects of your life, you need to make sure that the list is still topical and relevant. Consider the statement that accompanied each Stocktake and make sure any major imperatives are included in a revised Really Personal Information. For instance, if you've uncovered a sadness that you've lost touch with an old friend, add it into regrets; if you've decided you really do want to train for a new career, put it in your wish list; if you feel depressed about the prospect of death, put addressing your feelings into the list of things you could use more time to do. The Really Personal Information page has to be fully comprehensive.

The process of doing the Audit will have helped to inform the contents of that page. The first version you wrote at the very beginning may be a shadow of this latest one, and there may well be elements of the original that you can delete because they are no longer relevant. This might be because they have been resolved along the way or because, now that you have gained a better understanding of your life, you can see that they are not really regrets or dreams you need to address.

As well as honing that regrets list and wish list you should also have a much better understanding of who *you* are and what makes you happy or sad.

Ask yourself these questions:

- *Do you like yourself any better?*
- *Do you feel any sense of sympathy for the person whose life you've been scrutinising and who might have been in a muddle?*
- *If initially you felt somewhat depressed at the way your life was looking under that scrutiny, are you feeling any more cheerful now that you've eliminated the chaff?*
- *Are you looking forward to making more of life and of yourself?*
- *Are you wondering where on earth you are going to start?*

The answer to all the above should be 'yes'. Yes, you *should* like and care more about yourself, if for no other reason than the fact that you have been so honest about the mismatch between reality and aspiration. You *should* be excited that you've cleared space and time for some new plans to grow, and of course that *should* be exciting even if you feel right now that, with all those disposable hours to fill, you could possibly drown in the sea of opportunity before you've taken even the first tentative paddle towards the new you.

Having identified the time you have to play with, the key now is to harness the strengths and skills at your disposal. You've spotted the potential time margins in your day – now you've got to check out your own armoury of ability. Even if you are still feeling uncertain about yourself and about what you want your life to be, take time out from all-encompassing self-appraisal and for just a few minutes accentuate only the positive. Practical, professional and personal skills and strengths, accompanied by confidence, a sense of enquiry and some resilience, are all you need to move forward. You don't need much of any of them – but you do need them *all*, and having looked at your life in the round you should find them all present and correct.

Ask yourself these questions:

- *What are your character strengths?*
- *What practical skills do you have?*
- *What professional skills do you have?*
- *What do you think other people like about you?*
- *What are the self-reliant aspects of your personality?*
- *Have you come through some adversities in the past?*
- *Are you feeling receptive to trying new things?*
- *Have you got enough spirit of enquiry to open new doors you come across?*
- *Have you convinced yourself it won't be the end of the world if some doors slam shut?*
- *Are you confident that no one is going to die if you hear the word 'no' or experience any other sort of rejection?*
- *Are you relaxed about the fact that some changes for the better may take longer than others?*

The Reference chart that follows is your opportunity to write an upbeat report on yourself. You are a unique combination of skills and attributes – there is no one else like you. So you have to make sure you don't miss anything and that you give yourself a glowing and comprehensive report. Acknowledge every single character strength you possess and every single area of wisdom gained from life experience. Translate *all* of it into one big positive resource pool of expertise. Everything counts – even bad experiences or unhappy times. In fact, in many cases those will be the very incidents that have equipped you with extra-special strengths and insights. If you have survived a really unhappy childhood, adjusted your career ambitions when you've failed exams, brought up a child on your own, coped during your own or others' illnesses, faced your creditors in a bankruptcy hearing, lost a partner or persevered during depression, then you have already tested your reserves and flexed your inner strengths against adversity. Just think how empowered you will be when you turn those abilities towards realising positive things.

And it's not just the *big* life challenges that are important; the little things matter too. If you are a parent, don't you think there should be a Nobel Peace Prize for the skills learnt when negotiating with teenagers? And no amount of leadership courses could tell you what you already know if you've successfully motivated a child to do their homework without question. If you are over 60, how dare anyone say you are set in your ways! With technological advances in recent years, from the Internet to barcode shopping, you have had to gallop to keep up compared with any previous older generation. You are therefore more proactively flexible and adaptable than most other age groups – with, of course, the added advantages of life experience and wisdom, which can't be purchased at any price. Whoever you are and whatever your age, now, with the prospect of new challenges, you need to reinforce what you have to offer as core strengths in order to spot and realise your full potential.

FILLING IN YOUR REFERENCE

- *See chart 38.*
- *Step outside yourself and view yourself objectively.*
- *Using only positive words, describe your personality, e.g. kind, caring, compassionate, intuitive, funny, interested, bright, clever, active, generous, concerned, brave.*
- *List your job/professional qualifications.*
- *List positive experiences gained in the workplace, e.g. learning the ropes as a junior in a team, trusted with responsibility as head of department, creativity sought as developer of ideas, loyalty and integrity respected as support to management, diligence and efficiency acknowledged when put in charge of checks and controls, efficacy and reliability endorsed when acting as facilitator.*
- *List your life experiences, e.g. youngest in large family, mother of two, divorced father of three, single person, have travelled, relations with mental health problems, have coped with lifelong asthma, home owner, member of sports teams, have coped with racial prejudice, have survived parents' divorce when young, active in community affairs, have been made redundant, great gardener, dropped out of college, do all own DIY, have been declared bankrupt and get by despite negative credit rating, so thrifty that you save enough out of the housekeeping to take the family on holiday; the list is endless. . . .*
- *List the abilities these experiences have proved you possess, e.g. organised, calm under pressure, non-judgemental, a good friend, good at customer relations,*

> *good at motivating others, great phone manner, writes good letters, good back room operator, good team leader, good team player, resourceful, practical, hands-on, flexible, loyal, entrepreneurial, imaginative, pragmatic, caring, diligent, supportive, efficient, inventive, resilient, confident.*

This is an exercise to reassure you, that despite the various challenges your wish list of ambitions may be about to set you, you have many strengths to call upon and much potential to exploit. The greatest attribute of all, however, is confidence in yourself: not only confidence that you are going to give these challenges your best shot, but also confidence that you won't let yourself be knocked back when things don't go according to plan. The fact that you took on the challenge of doing the Audit and looking closely at your life should be enough proof that you are a strong, resilient and determined individual who is prepared to deal with life's unpredictability, and, equipped with in-depth self-knowledge, to apply the same determination to realising your full potential.

Investment Opportunities – planning a better future

You have now identified the things you want to achieve or address in your life, the time you have available to do so, and the basic abilities and skills you can draw upon. Next, you have to plan how you are going to go about it because obviously you can't go hell for leather to realise all those dreams at once. So you need to categorise them and come up with an overall game plan that prioritises and then allots time investments to different aspects of your future.

I don't know what your dreams and ambitions are so I can't tell you how much time each is going to need to progress. What I can recommend, however, is a step-by-step approach that will invariably work. Your dream may not come true overnight, your life issue may not be instantly resolved – but an advancement towards resolution, however slight, will feel fantastic.

Filling in your Investment Planner

Now that you're well into the third stage of the Life Audit, things are really coming together: it's time to get creative with your chart filling! First, think back to the categories you used during the Daily Time Logs and Stocktakes. Can you prioritise the areas of your life into a list that starts with the most important and ends with the least important? Write down the categories in descending order on the Investment Planner (chart 39). Then, simply transfer into the appropriate categories the things you wrote down on your Really Personal Information sheet.

Start now by choosing one of your wishes, dreams, ambitions or things you would address if you had more time. Start small! Because while you might have decided that ultimately you want to move house and change jobs, sorting out your fitness or tracking down an old friend may well be quick wins that will encourage you to take on bigger projects. You have to grow the confidence in your own ability in order to effect changes in your life successfully, and so establishing a little track record won't hurt.

Now, how easy is it to think what would bring that wish closer? If it's something that seemed impossible in the past because you didn't have the time you will know now whether that's still the case. Look at your diary to discover where you could now fit it in, including any associated preparations or travelling, and commit to making it happen. Schedule it and do it! There! Sorted! Tick that box!

Filling in your Investment Account

But what about moving forward on the wishes that required more thought than just finding a *little* time to commit? Start to fill in your Investment Account chart 40. This is effectively your savings bank account. Remember the disposable hours you identified? That's the currency you have to play with, and this bank account is going to be where you chart the bigger time investments you make in realising your dreams. After you take each step towards realising something on your wish list, enter the time investment you have made here.

Use one sheet per wish or ambition. Now think of one action, however small, that might bring your wish just that tiny bit closer. In fact at this first stage, the smaller that first step the better. Don't worry about whether it's the right or the wrong first step – finding out that that action got you nowhere is just as likely to point you in the right direction that *will* move you forward. Any action is going to be a good action – and is certainly a great improvement on the situation only a

Third Stage

227

short while ago when you did nothing at all about improving your lot.

Next, look at the action you have decided upon and make a best guess at the amount of time that first step is going to take. Write it in. All you have to do now is to turn to your diary or diary worksheets and identify where you are going to have time to carry out the action and so make that investment. Adjust the figure you entered in your Investment Account for the actual time the action takes. You will find as you carry on this exercise that you will become increasingly proficient at judging the amount of time certain activities will need.

At the end of a sequence of steps there is room to calculate the total time you have invested which needs to be transferred to the recalculation of overall time being spent across all your wishes, which happens on the overall Investment Bank Account Statement (chart 41).

Filling in your Overall Statement

This should list the total time spends on each and all the dreams and ambitions you are spending time trying to achieve. It has space for you to record your opening balance at the top, i.e. Z – your total available time, once you're improved your Stocktake Breakeven figures, and then a closing balance at the bottom, which is what you have left once you've totted up the amount of time you need to invest in your dreams and subtracted it from Z. This is your means of keeping track on your fluctuating stock of 'dream time'.

Trading Adjustments – making informed changes

Now let's look more closely at those steps you need to take. Thinking about the *first* steps to take shouldn't have been too difficult. If the dream has been one you have held for any length of time you probably knew the first thing you were going to do about it when you had time.

If it's a *life* issue or problem that you have determined to devote more time to you may already have a plan of campaign to, say, spend more one-on-one time with a person with whom you have a troublesome relationship. You need to build that in across a period of time to make sure it happens and really commit that time investment.

But what if your wish needs more informed or specialist knowledge and you are not sure where to start on the journey to realising it? To move forward you need to get equipped with professional guidance or to reap the benefit of others' experience. In this case, your first step is most likely to be information-gathering. It could be as simple as looking something up on the Internet, in the telephone directory or at the library. Getting hold of the right information is very important. You've done all the groundwork to free up time to work on this plan of yours – it would be catastrophic if you set off to realise it unprepared.

You are going to treat the exercise of getting some of those wishes granted with the same sort of meticulous attention to detail that you've been employing to stocktake and audit your current situation. You didn't rush into finding out your life Breakeven positions without doing research into the current reality. Nor are you now going to consider yourself informed enough to career headlong into wish fulfilment without equipping yourself with the relevant facts and figures, considering your options and all the stages of the process, and then relating all this up to the time you have available and the effects it might have on any other aspect of your life.

Really think about the sources you can access to find out everything you need to know. Once you've thought of them, think some more – *laterally*. Start with yourself. Don't forget the little voices inside you that you tuned into to hear better. Keep listening to what they tell you, especially if it's to do with changing direction, or with new developments that affect a plan. Be alert to those messages. What might have seemed a good idea when you wrote it down on your original wish list might not, on reflection, seem such a splendid plan after all.

Let's say you are like Shaun, 27, talented, with an interesting job as an illustrator in an advertising agency. He likes his job well enough, although he enjoys working on some accounts better than others and feels that he's not paid enough and that his prospects with this particular firm are limited. The projects he most enjoys, predictably, are the ones that reflect his own interests in extreme sports and activities. Outside work one of his big loves is music, and increasingly he wonders whether he shouldn't try to get a job in that industry.

He's feels he's floundering and indecisive. Having carried out the Audit, however, he also understands that it is imperative he addresses the problem and enters 'getting more career satisfaction' and 'earning more money' on his wish list, fully aware that if he doesn't do something it could end up on his regrets list.

So he's heard his inner voice, which is getting increasingly insistent, and now has to make a move. The first thing is to find out what opportunities there might be in his areas of interest. For him it's the music business, extreme sports and the advertising clients and campaigns he has enjoyed working on. The next time he goes to a music festival he does more than just watch the bands. He takes note of the business end of the gig, who the sponsors are, how it's organised, the names on the programme and posters of those involved in the various aspects of the event. What he's looking for are paid jobs for which he might have the appropriate skills. He talks to his boss at the agency about working only on the specific types of account he enjoys most. He researches those clients' businesses to find out more about them and what other suppliers they use, and he finds out about the career paths of people who are in positions in which he himself would like to be in the future.

This first part of Shaun's journey was purely fact-finding, but it proved to him how many different avenues he could go down and how wide the opportunities were. He ended up realising there was a wealth of opportunity out there and that he had to make some more decisions about what he was going to pursue and how. He is now researching the idea of setting up his own business enterprise to make the most of his skills and experience in bringing sport, music and commerce together in a promotion and sponsorship role.

So research is the key. First Shaun listened to himself, then he talked to as many people as he could in the areas he was interested in. Start close to home and think about your family, friends, colleagues and acquaintances. If you had knowledge or skill in a particular area and someone

Third Stage

asked your advice you'd give it, wouldn't you? Each of the people you know will have something to offer – could it be relevant or helpful to you? Don't forget to think beyond people's paper or work qualifications. Just like you, they have a well of life experience to draw on.

Always try to talk to someone who has been there and done whatever it is you are setting out to achieve. There is nothing quite like having a friend in an alien camp. If you chance upon an exceptionally friendly or helpful stranger during your investigations, prime them for future contact by asking them if they'd mind you coming back to them if you have any further queries.

The Internet is a fabulous tool, although it can also waste hours of time if you don't hone your search areas. Learn to use it efficiently. Read the Help or Search tips and add any really relevant sites to your Favourites list.

Don't forget to look closer to home as well. There is sure to be a book related to your dream, so find it. Your local library or telephone directory may have details of local groups, organisations or individuals who can help further your dream. Opportunities can crop up in the most unexpected places, so keep your eyes and ears open. Tom wrote on his wish list that he wanted to learn to sing opera. He lives in a remote village, but was astonished to see a card in the local post office window placed by a retired international tenor who was offering private lessons.

The Investment Project Management chart will help you track your actions, and I recommend you start a file of research notes for each investment subject, perhaps sticking the form on the cover as a quick reminder. As you explore one avenue so other options are likely to appear, and you may decide to go off on a tangent. Just typing in the subject name of your dream into your websearch will yield a multitude of related subjects.

Filling in your Investment Project Management chart

See chart 42. Write down the subject area of your particular plan and the date. Enter your start date and the date by which you would hope to have completed the project. Articulate your goal and why you are pursuing it. Think hard about the elements and information you need to collect in order to understand fully what needs to be done. Start researching and write down the contact details of information sources, the date and whatever information was gleaned in the Notes column. Come to a conclusion, which should include any revisions to your original goal and then start your action plan, itemising what you do and when and adding comments as you go. The 'Other considerations' space is for you to note any other areas of your life that might be affected by actively pursuing a course of action, and might accordingly need to be considered.

Chronicle your journey and make notes of other opportunities you may want to pursue at a later date. Keep a list of useful telephone numbers and addresses. Every time you talk to anyone or the address specifies a named individual write that name down – nothing beats talking to a real person, and it is always best to go back to someone you've already spoken to if you need more advice or assistance.

However anxious you are to get going on actually *doing* something towards your dream, hold back until you are

Third Stage

convinced you are as informed as you can be. Make sure that dossier of yours is complete and comprehensive. If it contains a range of options or courses to choose from, have them tabled ready for consideration when you have collected all the facts. Only then are you ready to decide how you are going to proceed. Perhaps when you wrote that wish down all those days ago it was a pie-in-the-sky fantasy. Now, faced with the cold facts, you will know whether it is potentially achievable and what it will take to get there.

Ask yourself these questions:

- *Will you be able to progress your plan in the free hours you know you've got?*
- *Or are you going to have to make adjustments in other areas of your life to accommodate it?*
- *Will it require extra funds?*
- *Will it affect any relationships?*
- *Does it involve travel or being in a different location? What knock-on time effects will there be?*
- *Does it require you to be fitter?*
- *Will it affect your image/wardrobe?*
- *Has the research prompted any shifts in your attitudes or opinions that you are aware of?*

If you still hold the dream dear after carrying out your research, you are about to fit it into your life and bank a lot of time in that particular investment account. That will mean you are going to make adjustments to the structure of your life, as established at the Breakeven point. Realising that dream, and the actions that it will require, are items that are about to join the rest of your commitments as a fact of life. So before you proceed you need to make those adjustments to your life Balance Sheet, fully informed about the effects on other areas of your life, the time your plan is going to take and when you are going to be carrying it out.

Reconciliation – facing up to facts

Facing up to facts is exactly what you've been doing all the way through the Audit. You have been honest with yourself about everything, and it's really important that you continue to be so now that you are moving forward. Equally important is to establish a routine of reconciliation, making sure the various components of your life, both facts and fantasies, balance and add up.

You have now built a formal place in your life for your ambitions. You have a system at your disposal to make them more than just things on your wish list. The same holding place is there for your regrets and sadnesses too, so that you can acknowledge them properly and work out how and when you are going to deal with them.

Regrets are things you either have to make better or let go. What you can't do is continue to let them blight your life. What's past is past. If you are struggling with regrets and don't see how you can go back and make things better, or find closure, then you could try a process that works in reverse to the system you have used with your wishes.

Filling in your Regret Reconciliation form

Using chart 43, and giving over one sheet to each regret, write down what it is you have regrets or sadness about. Make your starting point the moment that marked the beginning of the regret. Write that date down, and then trace the events and occurrences that have marked each stage in the realisation that your actions at that moment, and subsequent ones, are now being experienced as regrets.

Your regret may be about some opportunity that came along earlier in life and that you didn't pursue. Missed education and failing to do something creative such as paint, write or dance were regrets mentioned over and over again by Life Auditors. As they nearly all discovered, it is never too late to learn! However, if your regret is more personal or connected with a relationship that went wrong, look back and consider carefully whether there is some aspect of it that could be put right now. What solutions can you come up with? What would make everything all right if you could wave a magic wand? An apology, talking about it, an opportunity not taken then that might still be open now? Is there *anything* you can think of that will in any way lessen the load of this particular regret for you or any others involved? If there is a possible solution, what is preventing you applying it? Write down the obstacles and think about why they are preventing the resolution of this problem.

You can't think of a solution? Why not? If you can only think of obstacles, write them down one by one and really stare at them to double-check that there is definitely, absolutely, nothing that you personally can do at this moment to put things right. Think of those resources again. Do you need to reinforce your knowledge or experience here? Remember the tools – your inner voice, your family and friends, your determination to ask questions in order to get answers. Any help there? Write down any positive things you can do to remedy the problem. Really consider what *you* have got to lose if you are concerned about taking a particular course of action. Pride, rejection, failure – are any of them worse than not having a go at removing the past regret?

Still can't see a way to make things better? In that case, can you let this sadness go? Can you write down a case for closure? Having done the best you can to make it better, can you fold up that bit of paper and put it away for good? You've done your best, the moment has well and truly passed and it's time to move on unencumbered by something you now know you can't change.

If this is still a struggle, you may decide that it is such an important issue in your life that you need a professional to help you. While auditing your life is all about taking control and responsibility for your own mindset, calling in the experts has been suggested in other areas, and this one should be no different if you've tried all other measures without success. Turn your investigations into finding the right expert – someone with qualifications, reputation and experience appropriate to the area of your regret. Use those tools again to find this person.

Cyril knew that he was still grieving for his brother who had died a year previously. 'What I hadn't fully realised, though, was that I felt guilty that I hadn't supported him more. He was an alcoholic, and as a family we all tried to sweep it under the carpet. The booze got him in the end, and I know I could have done more.' But Cyril was making reparation by caring for his late brother's disabled son and taking responsibility for his future security. 'It's my way of dealing with the regrets I have about not doing more before.'

With final resolution of regrets and active realisation of wishes you have now achieved a level of life reconciliation; you literally have the measure of your life. You have a clear and informed picture of your life demands and the time they take up. It's really important that you continue to reconcile by matching your expectations with reality and, as your life changes, by making sure those adjustments are reflected in that bottom line figure of the disposable hours available to you. Be honest about failures and about those planned actions that don't happen.

Become a Life Entrepreneur – now you've got real, be brave

If you are keeping an informed balance in your life and reconciling your metaphorical books continuously, you should be feeling optimistic about your future opportunities. If, however, you are like Geraldine, who found it difficult to work out exactly how she wanted to make her life better, and your wish list was also skimpy, you may be unsure how to invest hours in any particular plan to make your life better, more exciting or more fulfilling. Don't despair – be brave. Make the task of identifying something that you really want to do one of the items on your wish list and research it along the lines suggested. Presumably you have pinpointed, minimised or eliminated factors in your life that make you unhappy, so now you need to pinpoint, maximise and introduce factors that are the reverse.

While the Audit has set out from the beginning to stress the importance of acknowledging the significance of the little things in life and how they can affect our happiness, now is the time to think big too. Most of us have at least one big ambition and talk about it as though it was within our reach, while knowing deep down that we'll never get near achieving it because it would involve too much turmoil and disruption. You know the sort of thing: 'One day I'll own that big house . . . learn to fly . . . be famous . . . take a year off to go travelling . . . move to the country . . . open a restaurant,' and so forth.

Our family and friends have probably indulged us in our fantasies as the years have passed, and we dredge up those pipe dreams time and time again. Now is the time to move beyond the talking shop. Why not apply exactly the same principles of research and enquiry to move one step nearer your *big* idea? What can it hurt? Have a go. You'd be surprised how some things, however outlandish, can be within your grasp after all.

One of 55-year-old James's big regrets was not trying to play golf competitively and professionally when younger. He started to research the professional golf circuit competition classes and discovered a veterans' league that offered just as much of a challenge and kudos as the more youthful one. He is determined to raise his game enough to compete, and is now planning to take early retirement from his accountancy partnership to devote himself to his new plan full-time.

Jackie and Paul had felt too committed to providing a stable home for their three children for Paul to give up his job as a sales director in a chemicals company. However, once their youngest had taken his GCSEs and opted for a trade apprenticeship they decided the time had come to chase their long-held dream of travel. 'We've decided to take a grown-up gap year and drive a motor caravan on the Continent,' said Jackie. 'We want to look into setting up some sort of import business which would give us an ongoing reason to have a travel aspect to our life. We don't know what yet – handicrafts perhaps, fabrics or maybe even food. We'll have plenty of time on this first trip to talk about it, though.'

Georgie and Martine, both in their early thirties, decided to put some serious research into the catering business. Secretaries in a law firm, they shared a passion for cooking. When a local bistro came up for sale near their office they decided to look into what would be involved if they bought it. It was nowhere near as complicated as they thought: they scrutinised the figures, studied the competition and established that they would be able to raise enough money against their flats. Within weeks they had made the decision to take the plunge. 'It's a big step for both of us, but neither of us have got any big commitments and we just felt we'd be mad not to have a shot at it.'

Whatever your dream or ambition, you must explore what it would take to try to make it happen. You've got all the tools to help you make the right decisions, so go on – now you've got real, be brave!

Credit Rating – take it where it's due and play to your strengths

I asked lots of people who had carried out the Life Audit what the process had felt like. Liberating and empowering, sometimes unsettling and shaming, revealing and surprising, intensely private and personal were some of the descriptions. The overwhelming effect it seemed to have, however, was that of giving people confidence: confidence in themselves and also greater confidence in the decisions and actions they were taking, both at a day-to-day level and on the bigger plans they might be instigating.

You have no reason to be reproachful of yourself or your life. By being as honest as you have been you have proved that you are not going to take any level of discontent lying down. That is a great achievement in itself. You may not be able to solve all your problems – you have to accept there is an ebb and flow to life, and of course you'll be dealt blows and suffer setbacks just like everyone else. But every setback should teach you something, and in some cases you will need to get some things wrong in order to discover how to get them right. Anyway, you now have a system to help you deal with it and you have put in the legwork to make sure that, whenever you can, you make a measured and appropriate decision when faced with either opportunities or dilemmas. Being shored up in this way is like having a ready savings account that you can draw upon when needs must. That fact alone should give you confidence and prepare you for just about anything life throws at you.

You've got through life in a freefall fashion up to now,

Third Stage

without a plan. Now, not only do you have a game plan but you also know much more about who you are. You've faced up to your faults, you've been doing something about them and you've acknowledged your strengths, too. So, just as you would advise someone else, or just as you would if you were in business – play to those strengths. They are being employed to facilitate your investments in your dreams; they are part and parcel of that credit-rich savings account that will help you face future challenges; and they are yours to call upon. So play to them, and take credit where it's due!

Takeover Target – live life on your terms and don't be ambushed

Something not so nice now – sorry. There's a tiny downside to the lovely contented and confident life you should now be embracing. Be prepared for some other people not to feel so jolly about your new-found focus! There you are – all self-contained and looking forward to making the most of yourself and your life – when you hear a faint bleating of, 'But what about me? . . . What about us?'

Alexis had felt very deflated by her parents' response to her new-found enthusiasm to retrain as a teacher when she established how bored she was working in a city centre estate agency. 'I'm only 30, but they made me feel positively geriatric and said I was too old to start again. I think their attitude stemmed from concern about me giving up a well-paid job with security, but I was disappointed they weren't more supportive.'

The opposite happened when 55-year-old Steve decided to take voluntary retirement from his management job. 'My 14-year-old daughter was obviously put out. I think she thought that was the end to our summer holidays abroad and her allowance.' Several Life Auditors reported their partners' anxiety about change clouding the exciting futures they were mapping out, and when you think about it it's hardly surprising, is it?

Other people may have liked you just as you were, thank you very much, and may find the new you rather off-putting or alarming, especially if you are thinking about changing things. Remember, they are not party to the journey of exploration you have been carrying out. You may not even have felt able to tell them about the analysis to which you exposed your relationship with them. But assuming you haven't decided to write them out of your life, there really is no justification for their feelings of insecurity. Do your best to reassure them: just don't let them stop you in your tracks, make you abandon your plans or ambush your life. Especially if you are someone who has taken responsibility for others' happiness as well as providing for their practical needs, you may find your plans being hijacked by what they see as their claim on you.

The role of looking after them, the part you play in their lives, even if it's passive time, just 'being there' time, can be just as invasive of your ambitions. You may find your plans being taken over by others' needs, and you may have to go back and reaudit that relationship and reassess the commitment and maintenance it requires. But be aware that what you are experiencing may simply be another person's reaction to the new, focused, life-efficient you. Much as others may profess to care for you and want the best for you, they may primarily be worried about their own status in the relationship and may be less than generous in encouraging you to forge ahead with your personal plans.

Encourage them too to carry out the Life Audit, so that they can profit from the experience themselves and understand the progression you've been through. Distract them by getting them to redirect their interest in your plans towards themselves and their own dreams and ambitions. Help them, support them, do whatever you know (because you *do* now know) that the relationship needs or warrants. Just don't let them ambush you!

Profit and Loss – keep assessing this new life and this new you

More often than not, successful people are the flexible, adaptable ones who don't get hung up on one particular aspect of their business or enterprise and who are receptive to change and open to fresh opportunities. They also spot when moments have passed and sell-by dates reached. You need to consolidate the hard work you have put into your life by adopting an open mind about future needs and changes.

The main certainty about all aspects of life is its *un*certainty. This unpredictability will bring as many blessings as miseries and the slammed doors and shifts in your fortunes will cause a waterfall effect into all areas of your life. You'll have to let chaos into your life occasionally, when events rather than plans dictate what happens. It would be very negative to resist spontaneous happenings that make you adjust or adapt, because often the best opportunities turn up out of the blue.

You've done the groundwork of stocktaking your basics, and now you need to make renewed assessment part of your schedule annually, twice a year or whenever you feel the need. It's up to you to decide how often you want to revisit the Audit, but *do* revisit it to stay aware and alert to those inner voices. Future assessments will need nowhere near as much detailed work. Finding your Breakeven position will be more a matter of amendment than itemising, and increasingly the 'must-haves' and 'must-dos' will be whittled down to a uniform amount that remains pretty static on all fronts.

Putting down on paper how to conduct your Life Audit has been an extraordinary experience for me, as has talking to so many people about the issues and insecurities they have to deal with. We are all completely unique and, while we are all to a degree dependent on other people, circumstance and fate, we are all essentially alone in dealing with life's bouquets and brickbats. We may have lesser or greater reserves of family, friends, qualifications and money, but only we know what is really going on inside our heads and hearts.

I suppose what I was trying to do when I invented the Audit for myself was to make my heart's desires match the space they could have in my life, because I didn't want to let anyone else down or turn my world upside down without really thinking about the issues involved. I wanted to work out how I and others would profit from any decisions I made, and to understand any potential loss in terms of the things or people I would have to let go from my life. At every stage I have had to reassess this because one shift in my life's pattern or one shift in my attitude has led to another and another . . .

Now my writing is finished, I can't wait to go back to my charts and Stocktakes and assess my life all over again. My objective when I came up with my plan all those months ago, sitting in bed with my men all gone, was not to write a book about the plan! But that was what happened and, incredibly, since then I've met and talked to all sorts of people about their lives. Some have gone travelling, some have taken early retirement or changed their jobs, some have started new businesses on their own, some have more love in their lives, some have chosen to have less. The one common factor is that all of them have changed things after considering how their current life matched the one they want to live.

Their experiences have shaped this book. The message is to be as honest with yourself as you can, be knowing and knowledgeable about your strengths and weaknesses, and be real about the 'must-haves' and 'must-dos'. Make sure you have them and do them, and only then move forward. Most important of all, as one thing leads to another, as it inevitably will, make sure you keep on reassessing and re-evaluating the resulting you from the profit and loss of your life actions.

It's only fitting, then, that you, the reader, should have the last word, and so the final chart (chart 48) in this book is for you to fill in the details of the new you. Remember your Personal Information and your Really Personal Information? How have you changed since then? This final chart is one for you to fill in with clearer, quite possibly different, facts, figures and priorities. It's a conclusive, indisputable situation report and final statement on you . . . until the next time!

THE
life ⊘
audit

charts

Me

Height

Weight

Skin tone

Eye colour

Hair colour   Length

Age   Date of birth

Distinguishing features

Health problems

Picture of myself

Family

Marital status

Dependants

Home

Address

Tel.   Mobile

Email

Type of accommodation

Work

Occupation

Business address

Tel.

Email

Annual income

Notes

If I had more time I would

-
-
-
-
-

I resent time spent on

-
-
-
-
-

I love spending time on

-
-
-
-
-

My regrets

-
-
-
-
-

My wishes

-
-
-
-
-

Notes

Daily Time Log

Date   Day

Notes

a.m.								Totals
1								
2								
3								
4								
5								
6								
7								
8								
9								
10								
11								
12								
13								
14								
15								
16								
17								
18								
19								
20								
21								
22								
23								
24								

What happened

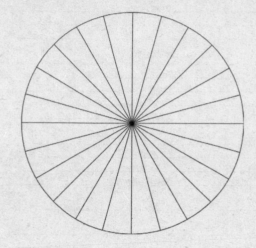

What should have happened

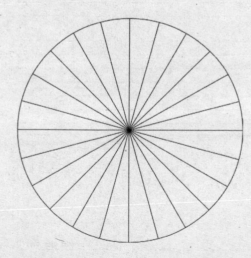

Key

☐ ....
☐ ....
☐ ....
☐ ....
☐ ....
☐ ....
☐ ....
☐ ....

Statement

I woke up today feeling _____ *about the day ahead*

because _____

Health

Health issues _____ Weight _____

Exercise _____

Supplements _____

Food

Breakfast _____ Beverages _____

Lunch _____ Alcohol _____

Supper _____ Cigarettes _____

Snacks _____ Diet units _____

Relationship – I spent time today with:

Special person _____ Friends _____

Family _____ Work colleagues _____

Acquaintances _____ Support/professional _____

Domestic chores

Work

Achievements _____

Frustrations _____

Money

Earned _____ Spent _____

Clothes

Leisure

Citizenship

Miserable moments

Blessings counted

Other

I went to bed feeling _____ *about the day*

because _____

Health Stocktake: Physical Wellbeing

Date

	Problem	Triggers	Impact & Management	Time req'd (d w m y)	Check-up frequency	Time req'd (d w m y)
Arms						
Back						
Blood pressure						
Bowels						
Breasts						
Cholesterol						
Ears						
Eyes						
Face						
Feet						
Hair						
Hands						
Head						
Heart						
Hips						
Intimate						
Kidney						
Legs						
Liver						
Lungs						
Mouth						

Problem	Triggers	Impact & Management	Time req'd (d w m y)	Check-up frequency	Time req'd (d w m y)
Muscles					
Neck					
Nose					
Skin					
Stomach					
Teeth					
Throat					
Other					

Statement

Audit period =

	sub total	x	total (audit period)	x	total (year)
daily (d)					
weekly (w)					
monthly (m)					
other (y) i.e. yearly, twice yearly					
Amount to transfer					

Health Stocktake: Physical Wellbeing

Date

Problem	Triggers	Impact & Management	Time req'd (d w m y)	Check-up frequency	Time req'd (d w m y)
Arms					
Back					
Blood pressure					
Bowels					
Breasts					
Cholesterol					
Ears					
Eyes					
Face					
Feet					
Hair					
Hands					
Head					
Heart					
Hips					
Intimate					
Kidney					
Legs					
Liver					
Lungs					
Mouth					

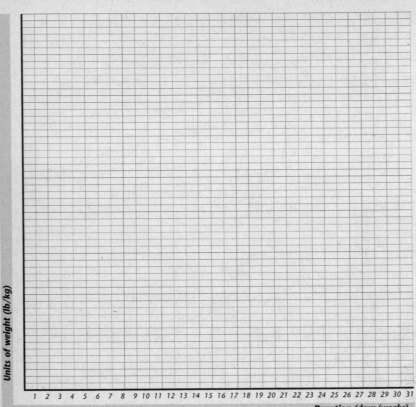

Units of weight (lb/kg)

1 2 3 4 5 6 7 8 9 10 11 12 13 14 15 16 17 18 19 20 21 22 23 24 25 26 27 28 29 30 31

Duration (days/weeks)

Statement

Date   Day

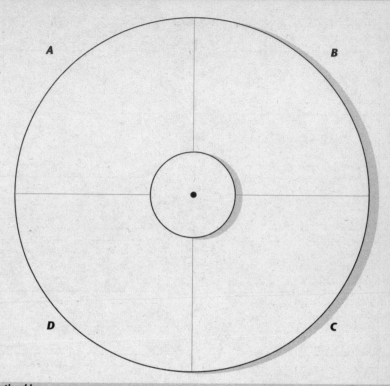

Relationships

A   B   C   D

_____   _____   _____   _____
_____   _____   _____   _____
_____   _____   _____   _____
_____   _____   _____   _____
_____   _____   _____   _____
_____   _____   _____   _____
_____   _____   _____   _____
_____   _____   _____   _____
_____   _____   _____   _____
_____   _____   _____   _____
_____   _____   _____   _____
_____   _____   _____   _____
_____   _____   _____   _____
_____   _____   _____   _____
_____   _____   _____   _____

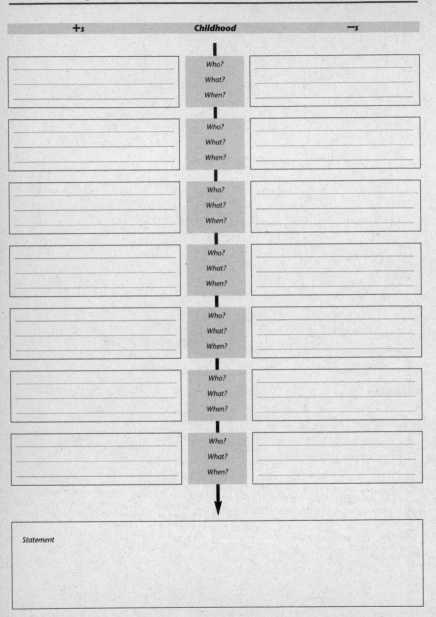

+s	Childhood	−s
	Who? What? When?	
	Who? What? When?	
	Who? What? When?	
	Who? What? When?	
	Who? What? When?	
	Who? What? When?	
	Who? What? When?	

Statement

Relationship Stocktake: Time and Needs

Date   No.

Who	Category	Sustenance	Dedicated time	Issues

Statement

Audit period =

	sub total	x	total (audit period)	x	total (year)
daily (d)					
weekly (w)					
monthly (m)					
other (y) i.e. yearly, twice yearly					
Amount to transfer					

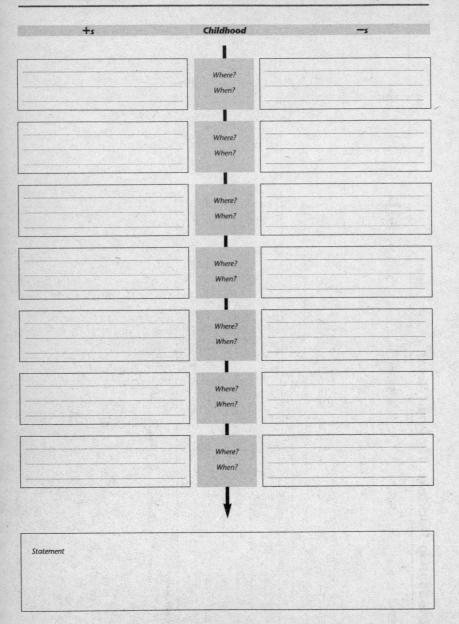

+s	Childhood	−s
	Where? When?	
	Where? When?	
	Where? When?	
	Where? When?	
	Where? When?	
	Where? When?	
	Where? When?	

Statement

Home Stocktake

Date   **Day**

Room

Contents
_____
_____
_____
_____
_____
_____
_____
_____
_____
_____
_____
_____
_____
_____
_____
_____

To buy or junk
_____
_____
_____

Outstanding jobs
_____
_____
_____
_____
_____

Cleaning – daily
_____
_____
_____
_____

Cleaning – weekly
_____
_____
_____
_____
_____
_____

Cleaning – monthly
_____
_____
_____
_____

Cleaning and maintenance – annually
_____
_____
_____

Other
_____
_____
_____
_____

Time
_____
_____
_____
_____
_____
_____
_____
_____
_____
_____
_____
_____
_____
_____
_____
_____

Audit period =					
	sub total	x	total (audit period)	x	total (year)
daily (d)					
weekly (w)					
monthly (m)					
other (y) i.e. yearly, twice yearly					
Amount to transfer					

Statement

Wardrobe

Occasions/events I need clothes for

_____
_____
_____
_____
_____
_____
_____
_____
_____
_____
_____
_____
_____
_____
_____
_____
_____
_____
_____
_____
_____
_____
_____
_____
_____
_____

Actual clothes worn

_____
_____
_____
_____
_____
_____
_____
_____
_____
_____
_____
_____
_____
_____
_____
_____
_____
_____
_____
_____
_____
_____
_____
_____
_____
_____

Audit period =

	sub total	x	total (audit period)	x	total (year)
daily (d)					
weekly (w)					
monthly (m)					
other (y) i.e. yearly, twice yearly					
Amount to transfer					

Statement

15   *Image Stocktake:* **Grooming**   *Date*

Grooming routines	Products	Frequency	Time
1			Daily Other
			Total
2			
			Total
3			
			Total
4			
			Total
5			
			Total
6			
			Total

Audit period =

	sub total	x	total (audit period)	x	total (year)
daily (d)					
weekly (w)					
monthly (m)					
other (y) i.e. yearly, twice yearly					
Amount to transfer					

Statement

Cuttings collection

Looks I like

Defining words

17 **Money Stocktake: Income and Expenditure** Date

Income		£
Wages /salary		
Tax credits/benefits		
Interest/dividends		
Other		
Total income		

Expenses		
House		
Utilities		
Shopping		
Cars		
Finance costs		
Travel		
Entertainment		
Sport/hobbies		
Children		
Pets		
Holidays/special occasions		
Other		
Total expenses		

TOTAL INCOME MINUS EXPENSES

Assets			Balance £
Fixed assets	£		
House			
Furniture/paintings/antiques			
Electrical			
Fixtures and fittings			
Car			
Other			
Total fixed assets		£	
Cash and bank accounts			
Current a/c (in credit)			
Savings a/c			
Cash drawer			
Money owed to you			
Other			
Total cash and bank accounts		£	
TOTAL ASSETS			£
Liabilities			
Credit cards/store cards			
1.			
2.			
3.			
Total credit and store card		£	
Other liabilities			
Current a/c (overdraft)			
Money owed (less than 1 year)			
Tax owed			
Other			
Total other liabilites		£	
Long-term liabilities			
Mortgage			
2nd mortgage/loan			
Car loans			
HP loans			
Other long-term loans			
Total long-term liabilities		£	
TOTAL LIABILITIES			£
NET WORTH + or -			£

Work Stocktake: Time Commitment & Job Satisfaction

Activity	1	2	3	4	5	6	7	8	9	10	11	12	13	14	15
10															
9															
8															
7															
6															
5															
4															
3															
2															
1															

Hours at work including travel

Audit period =

	sub total	x	total (audit period)	x	total (year)
daily (d)					
weekly (w)					
monthly (m)					
other (y) i.e. yearly, twice yearly					
Amount to transfer					

Statement

Job title

Official job description

Reality differences

Attainments

Failures

Who/what's bugging me

How do I think my bosses would describe me

Other

Work certainties/probabilities

3 months

6 months

1 year

5 years +

Statement

Time spent

Activity	Daily	Weekly	Other	Crossover	Added value

Totals

Audit period =

	sub total	x	total (audit period)	x	total (year)
daily (d)					
weekly (w)					
monthly (m)					
other (y) i.e. yearly, twice yearly					
Amount to transfer					

Statement

Activities

What	Time spent (d w m y)

Awareness

What	Scale	Theme/issue

Audit period =

	sub total	x	total (audit period)	x	total (year)
daily (d)					
weekly (w)					
monthly (m)					
other (y) i.e. yearly, twice yearly					
Amount to transfer					

Statement

Soul Stocktake   *Date*   *Day*

Beliefs

Spiritual ———————————————— Non-believer

Organised religion ———————————————— Personal worship

Personality

Optimistic ———————————————— Pessimistic

Lazy ———————————————— Workaholic

Gregarious ———————————————— Loner

Active ———————————————— Passive

Sexuality

Defined ———————————————— Undefined

High ———————————————— Low

Audit period =	sub total	x	total (audit period)	x	total (year)
daily (d)					
weekly (w)					
monthly (m)					
other (y) i.e. yearly, twice yearly					
Amount to transfer					

Statement

Mortality Stocktake

Thoughts about death

Often ———————————————————————— Never

Fear of dying

Great ———————————————————————— None

Belief in afterlife

Yes ———————————————————————— No

State of affairs – in event of death

Organised ———————————————————————— Disorganised

Statement

Balance Sheet

Total Hours Available (X)	Audit Period		Year	

Life areas	Time committed (audit period)	Time committed (year)
Sleep		

Total hours committed (Y)		

TOTAL TIME LEFT OVER (Z)		

Statement

Appointment on   *Date*   *Time*

Main symptoms

Duration of symptoms

Trigger conditions/medical history

Medication

Alternatives

Research

Notes

Fitness Planner

Date

	Monday	Tuesday	Wednesday	Thursday	Friday	Saturday	Sunday
a.m.							
1 Type of activity							
Intensity							
Time							
Other							
2 Type of activity							
Intensity							
Time							
Other							
p.m.							
1 Type of activity							
Intensity							
Time							
Other							
2 Type of activity							
Intensity							
Time							
Other							

Meal Planner

Date

	Monday	Tuesday	Wednesday	Thursday	Friday	Saturday	Sunday
Breakfast							
Lunch							
Supper							
Snacks							

Storage Inventory *Date*

Room
Name/description
General category of contents

Content	Description	Condition	Renew/update	Replace

Bakery and cakes	✓	Dairy	✓	Meat, fish, poultry	✓

Fruit		Vegetables		Ready meals	

Cereals, snacks, confectionery		Cooking/baking ingredients		Tins, packets, jars	

Soft and hot drinks		Alcohol		Household	

Toiletries		Pets		Other	

Housework Planner

31

Room	Daily	Weekly	Tasks Monthly	Other

Housework Rota Chart

Date

Person responsible

Chore/area	Mon	Tue	Wed	Thu	Fri	Sat	Sun

Room/space	Job	Frequency		
				As needed
				Monthly
				Spring
				Summer
				Autumn
				Winter

Decorating Chart

Room																																
Dimensions																																
Paint (woodwork)																																
Make/code																																
Colour																																
Type																																
Amount																																
Paint (walls)																																
Make/code																																
Colour																																
Type																																
Amount																																
Wallpaper																																
Make/code																																
Colour																																
Type																																
Amount																																
Flooring																																
Make/code																																
Colour																																
Type																																
Amount																																
Tiling																																
Make/code																																
Colour																																
Type																																
Amount																																
Curtains																																
Make/code																																
Colour																																
Type																																
Amount																																

Contact/details	Work no	Mobile no.	Other
Personal			
Home/Domestic admin			
Cleaner			
Appliance repair			
Plumber			
Builder			
Electrician			
Local council			
Local tip			
Garage			
Bank			
Accountant			
Solicitor			
House and contents insurance			
Other			
Work			
Key contact			
Personnel			
Other			
Health			
Doctor			
Dentist			
Other			
Leisure			
Sports			
Social			
Other			
Image			
Hairdresser			
Beautician			

Wardrobe Inventory

Key: **N** (Need) • **R** (replace) • **M** (mend)

Footwear (shoes, boots etc.)	**Tops** (T-shirts, shirts, jumpers)	**Bottoms** (trousers, skirts)	**Outfits** (suits, dresses)
Underwear / sleepwear	**Formalwear**	**Muckabouts**	**Sportswear**
Outdoor (coats, macs etc.)	**Accessories** (hats, belts, bags)	**Jewellery**	**Other**

In the Event of My Death   *Date*

I would like   **Burial / cremation / other**

To notify

Executor's name _____

Tel. _____

_____

Executor's name _____

Tel. _____

_____

Funeral director _____

Tel. _____

_____

Solicitor _____

Tel. _____

Donor Cards

_____
_____
_____
_____

Documents	Location
Will	
Birth certificate	
Marriage certificate	
Mortgage	
Life insurance policies	
Pension	
Share/investments certificates	
Loans and HP	
Building society passbooks	
Passport	
Bank	
Divorce papers	
Other	

Funeral service and wishes

Place of service _____

Type of service _____

Persons officiating _____

Music _____
_____

Readings/poetry – by whom? _____
_____

Particular responsibilities _____
_____
_____

Headstone _____

Flowers (if any) _____

Disposal of ashes _____

Notes

Personality

_____
_____
_____
_____
_____

Qualifications

_____
_____
_____
_____
_____

Work experience

_____
_____
_____
_____
_____

Life experience

_____
_____
_____
_____
_____
_____

Abilities/strengths

_____
_____
_____
_____
_____
_____
_____
_____

Category	Wishes, dreams, ambitions and regrets	✔
1	1	
	2	
	3	
	4	
2	1	
	2	
	3	
	4	
3	1	
	2	
	3	
	4	
4	1	
	2	
	3	
	4	
5	1	
	2	
	3	
	4	
6	1	
	2	
	3	
	4	
7	1	
	2	
	3	
	4	
8	1	
	2	
	3	
	4	
9	1	
	2	
	3	
	4	

Investment Account

Wish/ambition

Action steps	Estimated time	Actual time
	Total	

Investment Bank Account Statement   *Date*

Opening balance

Wishes, dreams and ambitions	Amount invested

CLOSING BALANCE

Subject

Date

Start date   **Estimated finish date**

Goal

Information needed

Research

Source	Date	Contact details	Notes

Conclusions

Action steps

Date	What	Notes

Other considerations

Regret

Date

Stages since regret started	**_Notes_**

Possible solutions	**_Obstacles_**

Action	**_Notes_**

Closure statement

Day Worksheet

Date   *Day*   44

Hours

1

2

3

4

5

6

7

8

9

10

11

12

13

14

15

16

17

18

19

20

21

22

23

24

Week Worksheet

Date   **Week**

Monday   *a.m.*   *p.m.*

Tuesday   *a.m.*   *p.m.*

Wednesday   *a.m.*   *p.m.*

Thursday   *a.m.*   *p.m.*

Friday   *a.m.*   *p.m.*

Saturday   *a.m.*   *p.m.*

Sunday   *a.m.*   *p.m.*

Month Worksheet

Date   Month

1	2	3	4	5	6	7
8	9	10	11	12	13	14
15	16	17	18	19	20	21
22	23	24	25	26	27	28
29	30	31				

Year Worksheet

No.   Date

January						

April						

July						

October						

February						

May						

August						

November						

March						

June						

September						

December						

Final Statement

I am a [ ] **year-old man/woman with these dependants and responsibilities**

_____
_____
_____
_____
_____

These areas of my life needed priority auditing and may need continuing review

_____
_____
_____
_____
_____

I know my weaknesses to be

_____
_____
_____
_____
_____

I believe my strengths to be

_____
_____
_____
_____
_____

In [ ] **months I want to have done/become/have/made**

_____
_____
_____

Longterm I want to do/be/have

_____
_____
_____

These are my priorities

_____
_____
_____

My motto/mantra/ethos is

_____
_____